HEELCATCHER

THE STORY OF JACOB REVISITED FOR THOSE WHO ARE ANXIOUS, TIRED, AND STRUGGLING TO MAKE LIFE WORK

STEVE FOSTER

Printed in the United States of America
First Printing 2019
First Edition 2019
ISBN: 978-1-07-204622-6

10 9 8 7 6 5 4 3 2 1

HEELCATCHER

To my four sons, Nate, Noah, Jonah, and Joshua:

May you be God-mastered men who prevail in this world.

Be still, and know that I am God;
I will be exalted among the nations,
I will be exalted in the earth!
The Lord of hosts is with us;
The God of Jacob is our refuge.
Selah

PSALM 46:10-11

TABLE OF CONTENTS

TABLE OF CONTENTS

PROLOGUE
WILD WATERS

I almost drowned.

Wild Waters.

Late 1970's.

I was around nine years old.

The whole family...all eight of us...loaded up in two cars and headed to the newly unveiled, newly opened Wild Waters in Ocala, Florida. It was a special treat. Waterparks were a fairly new concept. It was definitely new to our family. We rarely traveled anywhere...except to see family in Illinois or to go to an away Little League baseball game.

And our small town of Green Cove Springs, Florida offered little in the way of adventure.

We had a Pete's Hamburgers, a KFC, and a Pizza King. The Clay High Blue Devils' football and basketball games. Nine-hole golf at Reynolds Industrial Park. Fishing and shrimping on the St. Johns River. And the monkey bars, swings, and some kind of giant cheese structure in Spring Park.

And the Qui-Si-Sana, a cavernous spring that seemed like it meandered down into the watery belly of the earth. Supposedly it was once considered the Fountain of Youth. Now it was just a round pond in the middle of Spring Park...next to the pool...which was always too cold and too crowded to really enjoy.

Not that I liked the water.

I grew up in Florida but didn't really care for swimming. Maybe it was because the movie *Jaws* came out when I was young. Or maybe I just didn't like the thought of being underwater and knowing you could drown. But Wild Waters sounded like a trip to a magical land…almost like Disney World…and I couldn't wait to get there.

I can almost recreate the scene in my mind.

Large winding, intersecting bright blue slides. Red umbrellas hanging over picnic tables nestled under oak trees and newly built pavilions. People everywhere. The lovely smell of chlorine in the air.

After staking claim to one of the picnic tables, our whole family seemed to scatter.

I assume that I was with my brothers and sisters…or at least started off that way…but eventually, somehow, I ended up alone…standing in front of a giant pool.

I had never seen anything like it.

A massive sea of water that you could walk into…just like the beach…except with clear blue water, no sand, no menacing waves, and no Jaws. I mustered up my courage and made my way further and further into the deep end. Soon I was further out in the deep than I had ever ventured before.

Feeling brave. Feeling alive.

Then I heard these words over the loudspeaker.

"Here come the waves!"

I was confused and terrified at the same time as the water began to stir. Soon waves were developing all around me as people screeched in delight. I dog-paddled as fast as I could toward the side, hoping to get to a nearby ladder, but the waves kept pushing me away from it.

I did the next best thing in my mind.

I clutched onto a small side ledge about a foot below the edge of the pool.

I felt safe for a moment…until a wave of water crashed into my face.

Then another…and then another…

The wave buried my head in water and then passed by quickly, giving me a brief amount of time to catch my breath before another wave hit.

Stuck to the side of the pool. Paralyzed in terror. The waves kept coming.

The cold crash of water. The quick catching of a breath.

Water. Breath. Water. Breath.

I could see the waves coming one after another. Rhythmic. Endless. Relentless.

My breaths were getting quicker and quicker and harder and harder to time between the waves.

I started sucking in water.

I felt like I was drowning.

Then two arms reached down and grabbed me under the shoulders, pulling me to safety. I looked briefly at the older black man who had snatched me up from the water and then I darted off, choking out water and crying for my mom.

To this day, I don't know who he was…how he saw me…why he acted so decisively.

But I think he saved my life. Or at least saved me from a near drowning.

He probably forgot about it and moved on with his life. No one else saw his act, as far as I know. Perhaps he never said anything about it. In many ways, it probably wasn't a big deal in his mind.

But it is one of those events seared into my memory.

I still remember it. Remember him. Remember his act.

And I am extremely grateful.

Feeling like you are drowning is a terrifying experience.

Going underwater. Fighting for air. Thrashing in panic.

Wave after wave.

Struggling to breathe.

Sucking in water.

Breathing in fear.

Many years later, when going through my first bout of panic attacks, it would feel like I was drowning again.

But this time, there was no water.

I was drowning on dry land.

Still fighting to catch my breath.

Facing wave after wave of fear.

But this time, no one was around to snatch me up.

CHAPTER ONE
THE FIRST WAVE OF PANIC ATTACKS

O h, God, help me! Help me! Please help me!"

But God didn't answer.

The more I prayed that my anxiety would end, the more it seemed to swell in my soul.

My heart was racing. My mind was in full throttle. I felt trapped in a car going 120 miles per hour down a busy highway...but I was not driving. Something else was hurtling me down the road, and I could not stop. All I could do was anticipate the crash.

I knew the answers. I knew my thoughts were foolish, irrational, even stupid.

But I could not stop them. I was out of control.

It was a panic attack.

I knew the term. I had read about it. I had even counseled someone who experienced panic attacks. They were academic to me. Now they were real.

I was caught in one.

I couldn't breathe. I couldn't relax. I couldn't think straight. But somehow I *could* pray.

The problem was that I was tired of praying. It didn't work. In fact, it made things worse.

Whenever I recited Philippians 4:6-7 in my head...*Be anxious for nothing...but in everything by prayer and supplication, with thanksgiving...let your requests be made known to God... and the peace of God, which surpasses all understanding...*

will guard your hearts and minds through Christ Jesus... the anxiety increased... along with the guilt.

"What's wrong with me? Am I losing my mind?"

Prayer felt worthless. I felt worthless. Useless. And God felt useless to me.

This is a difficult thing to face when you are a pastor. And the reason you are panicking is because you have to stand in front of your congregation and preach the next day.

Was this the end of my ministry? Somehow I knew that, whatever happened, ministry for me would never be the same.

How did I get to this point? Let me backtrack...

From 1998-2010, I was the associate pastor at a church in New Jersey. Associate pastor can mean just about anything. In my case, it especially did.

I preached during the worship services. I taught at various times during the week. I counseled. I discipled. I led Sunday School. I led men's ministry. I oversaw children's ministries. I oversaw youth ministry. I organized small groups. I basically filled in wherever I was needed.

From marrying to burying. From fixing computers to praying with the sick. From overseeing nursery leaders to working with "senior saints." My ministry was often one of "filling gaps." And believe me...the typical church has a lot of gaps.

Ours certainly did.

Our church was a medium-sized Bible church of about 400 people in central Jersey. Started by a group of Conservative Baptist church planters in the 1950's, it had a rich history with devoted members and faithful leaders.

When I arrived at the church in 1998, it was my first time serving as an associate pastor. My first time living up north. My first time ministering to and with "Yankees."

Growing up in northeast Florida, going to school in Alabama, ministering as a youth pastor in Louisiana, I was accustomed to "southern culture." Slow. Friendly. Hospitable. Church-going. New Jersey was a change of pace. Life moved much, much faster. People were more insulated, occupied with work and long commutes. Church seemed to be an afterthought in the culture…a waste of time to many…something to squeeze into a tight schedule for the rest.

But my wife and I were excited about the challenge. It was a new adventure for us. We arrived in October 1998 just one month after our first son was born. We felt like missionaries, traveling out of our comfort zone, learning a new culture, and spending our first months living in an Italian family's basement until we could find a place of our own.

And the church responded well to us. They liked having a new family in their midst…and they loved our accents.

The first time I preached, I noticed several people snickering at various times during my sermon. Not in a disrespectful way. They just found my phraseology humorous. "Y'all." "Fixin' to." "Neck-ed" (pronounced "naked" up north). I didn't mind. It helped make the transition easier. They enjoyed laughing at me and I, in turn, found many reasons to laugh at "Yankees."

It was a good ministry marriage.

Seven years later, in 2005, my wife and I found ourselves in a small, adequate, somewhat charming 100 year-old home with three active young boys…and a fourth one on the way.

Ministry was going well, but it was also becoming discouraging. I had invested a substantial amount of time and emotional energy in reorganizing and reinvigorating our small group ministry. The climax came in the fall of 2004 with our church's journey through *The 40 Days of Purpose*. People came to faith. Excitement swelled. And forty small groups met throughout our local communities. The momentum was there. It seemed that our church would break past the "400 plateau," experience exponential growth, and transition into a fellowship-rich, small group-based, passionately-worshiping, evangelistically-dynamic church.

But the enthusiasm fizzled. The campaign ended. Thanksgiving and Christmas arrived. And by the New Year, everyone seemed more ready for rest than for revival.

I needed a break too. But I didn't take it.

The spring of 2005 saw me trying to manufacture momentum that was no longer there. I pushed small groups, but the excitement was gone. Nevertheless, I plodded forward, recruiting as many leaders and groups as possible…probably to keep myself from the embarrassment of going from forty small groups to four.

I also began to add more and more things to my plate. First came intense involvement in a young couple's life. They were new to our church. He was introverted but friendly. She was dying of cancer. My wife and I poured ourselves into their lives and gathered others to join us. With seemingly a few months for her to live, we were determined to make their last months together a time to remember. Literally a quarter of our time was invested in them—praying for them, being with them, traveling with them, counseling them, crying with them.

The emotional drain was more than I could imagine.

Second, we began work on an addition to our house. With our fourth son on his way, we were faced with one of three options: jam three young boys and a newborn baby into one small room, sell our house and buy a new one, or build an addition to our house. We chose option three and began the process of drawing up plans, storing up funds, working with the township, and finding contractors.

None of it came easily.

I am not mechanically inclined. I became the "general contractor" of our house addition because I liked saving money, not because I liked building things. I was swimming in unfamiliar waters, feigning aptitude in order to avoid being taken advantage of.

I did not succeed.

Pushy township officials, busy subcontractors, and failed inspections turned an 18' x 12' addition into a ten-month ordeal.

Our house addition was completed in September. Our child addition had already come in May.

Our fourth son, Joshua, is a major blessing…but in May 2005 he was a major stressor. We were not seeking a fourth child. Three young boys kept our lives busy enough. A fourth was not in our plans.

But God surprised us…as He often does.

The pregnancy shocked us both. I was convinced that the "unexpected blessing" must be my long-awaited daughter. Six months later, the ultrasound revealed otherwise.

As our Indian doctor relayed the news…

"It looks like you have a fourth son, Mr. and Mrs. Foster"…

I kept repeating halfway under my breath…

"Holy cow…holy cow….holy cow…"

Only as we left the doctor's office did my wife point out my potential lack of cultural sensitivity.

Joshua's arrival cast us back into the school of infant parenting. We had savored our graduation from this stage of life. No more baby food, poopy diapers, sleepless nights, or helpless little infants. Life was returning to some sense of normality. Our three boys—all eighteen months apart—operated pretty much on the same level. Eating on their own. Playing together. Getting ready for bed. Sleeping through the night. Joshua would be a "blessed interruption" to this routine.

At least we knew it was a blessing even if it didn't feel like one at the time.

One month after Joshua's birth, my wife's family rented a beach house in South Carolina. We drove down to join them. It was on this trip that we learned that Joshua did not like his car seat for more than ten minutes at a time. From New Jersey to South Carolina, we were treated to a non-stop serenade of screaming. My wife did all she could to console him—singing to him, rocking his seat, feeding him, reading to him.

Nothing worked.

After an hour of turning up the radio and tuning out the crying, I was ready to explode. It felt like a thousand needles were being jammed into my ears. We were all trapped. There was no escape. All I could do was make the most of it, get used to it, accept it…or scream in insanity and run the van off the road.

Thankfully I resisted this temptation. Barely.

Back in New Jersey, things weren't any better. Conflicts were erupting everywhere in our church. The biggest was between two of our leaders. Being friends of both, I was caught in the middle. I tried to understand both sides. I listened to the complaints, added my insights, worked toward peace. But the conflict deepened rather than lessened.

Discouragement hit…followed by disappointment…then disillusionment.

The church no longer seemed like a safe place to me. Under the smiles and pleasant greetings, I began to see hardened hearts, buried offenses, and bitter feelings.

The last item on my bulging plate was my doctoral dissertation.

I started attending Biblical Seminary in 2002. The Doctor of Ministry program was perfect for busy pastors. The campus was close, and I savored the extra input into my life. I have always enjoyed school and taking week-long classes at Biblical was more of a blessing than a burden. But as the classes came to an end, there was only one thing left on the academic agenda…the research, development, and writing of a doctoral dissertation. This task *did* seem like a burden to me.

They say that the journey of a thousand miles begins with the first step. Sounds nice, but the first step is not easy. All you can see at the beginning of the journey is a long, hot road over rocky terrain. Once you take that step, you know that you are in for a tiring, time-consuming, mostly unpleasant trip. So you stand there and stare, one part of you trying to convince your foot to move, the other part of you saying, "Isn't there a different road somewhere?"

A good number of graduate students never complete their doctoral degree because they never finish (or even start) their dissertation. I was determined not to be a "doctoral casualty." I almost became one anyway…not because of the dissertation itself but because of the shaky foundation that the stresses of life began to reveal in me.

The "perfect storm" was brewing and I simply did not see it coming.

The first crack in the dam occurred on a Sunday morning in the summer of 2005. I was preaching. Nothing unusual about that. I had preached my first sermon at age sixteen in a small Southern Baptist church in Florida. The rest of my life was practically centered on continuing to develop this gift.

But something happened that morning.

Right in the midst of speaking, I suddenly felt light-headed… disoriented…scared. I don't know which struck first—the emotional fear or the physical weakness—but once they showed up they worked together and amplified in intensity. Somehow I made it through. I kept on preaching without anyone in the congregation really knowing what was happening. The feeling may have only lasted thirty seconds or a minute. I can't remember. But the experience would be firmly imprinted on my mind. I had almost passed out in front of a congregation of 400 plus people, in the middle of a sermon, on a Sunday morning. Whoa.

As the associate pastor, I did not preach every week. The schedule usually had me at the pulpit every four to six weeks. During the four weeks until my next sermon, I found myself replaying the whole episode in my mind.

"What happened? What if I would have passed out? What would people think? What would people do? Would they rush up on the stage? Would they call an ambulance? What would happen next? Wouldn't that be a Sunday everybody would remember! Could I ever live it down?"

God gifted me with a good imagination. It is both a blessing and a curse at times. I can visualize things very well. Passing out in front of a congregation of people on a Sunday morning was something that I could vividly live out in my mind. No matter how I viewed it, it wasn't a pleasant picture. I could see the initial shock on people's faces. Confusion. An elder rushing up on stage. A deacon calling for an ambulance. A group of people huddled around me with water and cold rags. A whole service brought to a halt.

Where do you go from here?

Whenever the scene flashed in my head, I tried to squash it. But it kept coming back.

Soon the date arrived for me to preach again. On the stage again, I felt a similar feeling of panic and shortness of breath. I don't remember it being as intense. It was probably psychosomatic more than anything else. But a thirty second intrusion in a previous sermon was now moving in and taking up residence in my ministry life.

Months passed and the sermons kept coming. My anxiety level snowballed. I began to count the days until my next sermon with increasing dread and panic. I felt like a man on death row watching the hours tick until his execution. I know it sounds dramatic, but something precious to me was at risk.

I felt like I was drowning.

The emotional anxiety cropped up in physical ways. From the fall to the winter of that year, I developed strep throat on four separate occasions. My immune system was weak. My diet was suffering. My body was out of whack. But when my Sunday came to preach, somehow I kept getting up to speak and making it through two services. Only God knows how.

The breaking point hit in March of 2006. My emotions couldn't take it anymore. My body was worn down. My spirit was parched. My desperate prayers to God for inner peace remained unanswered. The more I tried to conquer my anxiety, the more it reared its ugly head. I was fighting a losing battle. My confidence was shot. My strength was gone.

As the date approached for me to preach, I could not stop the panic. The countdown in my mind began.

On Friday night, I actually thought about running my car off the road and getting in a "harmless" accident just so I would have an excuse for Sunday.

On Saturday, I did not even want to get up.

That night I was in full scale terror mode. I could not relax. My heart was racing. My mind was a blur.

That night I took two Tylenol PM pills in hopes of getting some sleep. Instead I found myself on the couch drifting back and forth between reality and a dream-like state…my body being unable to function but my mind being unwilling to rest. In the midst of this semi-conscious state, I remembered feeling like I was having a heart attack. I cried out for my wife, but the words would not come out. I tried to struggle to her, but I could not move. I did not know if I was really dying or not. When Sunday morning came, I wasn't sure which I preferred.

Relief finally came when I decided I could not do it. I could not preach. I would not preach.

I called a friend of mine, an elder at our church, and told him that I could not make it to church that day. He was somewhat aware of my struggles and was not totally surprised by my call.

My wife didn't fully understand but she stood by me. She gathered the kids together and went to church without me.

I laid on the couch, physically exhausted, emotionally drained, spiritually defeated. I had preached on stress on several occasions. I had counseled people with panic attacks. Now I was exposed as a hypocrite, a spiritual weakling, a failure to myself, to my family, to God.

I had no idea what the future held for me. For all I knew, my ministry had ended. Life as I had known it would never be the same.

"How can I continue when I can't even speak in front of people anymore? Who am I? How did I get here? Why I am so weak? So powerless? So worthless?" Something died in me that day. It would take me several months and years to finally discover what.

CHAPTER TWO
DRAWN TO JACOB'S WELL

When your world is rocked, you are faced with one of two choices.

Curl your soul into the fetal position. Draw in to yourself. Close out others. Build walls. Put up your defenses. Attack nosey intruders when necessary.

Or spread your arms open. Expose your heart for examination, for surgery. Look deep. Explore. Be vulnerable. Share. Allow the searchlight of God to shine in the recesses of your heart.

At first, I wanted to retreat.

Maybe this was the time to leave the church, leave ministry, or at least not care anymore.

When you are around Christians long enough, it is easy to become disillusioned. Rarely do you see true Christ-like love. Instead in the church there are often conflicts. Backbiting. Offended sensibilities. Grudges. I was tempted to put the blame for my anxiety and stress squarely on the backs of my fellow "brothers and sisters" in the Lord. I believed I was simply too sensitive of a soul to fellowship with critical, crotchety Christians.

But I knew that answer was too simple. This one was on me.

It was time to discover more about myself.

It is amazing how you can live with yourself, in yourself, and still not know yourself.

There were caverns in my heart that had never been explored. My emotional breakdown gave me the occasion to take a deep breath, turn on a flashlight, and figure out what lay beneath the surface of my life.

When you skip out on preaching a sermon, especially at the last minute, it raises questions in people's minds.

"Is Steve okay? Is he sick?"

A few individuals called to see how I was doing.

"I'm just not feeling well" was the only answer that I could manage.

It was true to an extent and it seemed to satisfy the curious and the concerned.

On the following Tuesday, I met with my senior pastor, Joe.

Joe is a hard-nosed, high "D" kind of guy (for those unfamiliar with the DISC personality profile, the "D" stands for dominant). Born in Philly. The son of a military man. Things are pretty cut and dry with Joe. Working with him in ministry had been a mostly pleasant experience. Our personalities balanced each other out. Joe is decisive but also wise and he learned to cater to my more laid back, relational style of leadership. For the most part, he "loosed me and let me go" in my areas of ministry with very little input or intrusion.

Coming into my office, he asked, "How did things go on Sunday?" He had just gotten back in town and apparently had not even heard what happened.

I was surprised.

"Not too well," I responded barely able to look at him.

"What happened?"

"I didn't preach."

For the next few minutes I tried to recount what was going on in my life. The story felt surreal as I told it…even though it was my own. Talking about it was humbling, but I had no choice. My eyes watered as I stammered through my words.

I was a broken man revealing my weakness to a man I perceived as strong and unfaltering.

His response caught me off guard.

"You feel like a failure, don't you?"

He hit the nail on the head. Wrap it all up...sum it all up...I felt like a failure.

I failed.

I failed to win the battle against my own anxiety. I failed to come through in the clutch. I failed my ministry. I failed my family. I failed my wife.

I failed God.

The way he asked the question assured me that he had some understanding of what I was going through. I guess that surprised me. In eight years of ministry together, up to that point, I had rarely seen the "soft underside" of Joe. We worked together, met weekly, discussed Bible passages, interacted...but never really went below the surface.

It is funny (and sad) how typical that is...even between mature ministers of the gospel of grace.

Joe encouraged me to see a Christian counselor. He recommended one. He offered to cover the expense. I was floored and encouraged.

A few weeks later I was at a counselor's office. I sat in an isolated room. Magazines were scattered on a small table. Well-framed, Thomas Kinkade-ish pictures were all around. The sound of a fan or some kind of ambient noise filled the room and kept the discussions going on in the nearby office private and secure.

Everything breathed…"Relax. You are safe here."

Dr. O, as I came to call him, spoke in the same kind of soothing way. Unhurried. Deliberate. Calming. I found myself analyzing the situation as much as myself.

"So this is how you counsel people. Make everything calm and relaxed. Ask good questions and just listen."

Nothing earth-shattering came out of my meetings with Dr. O. I can't think of too many things he said that really helped. But it gave me an opportunity and permission to explore my own heart. He served as a sounding board, a guide of sorts. As the light shined into the cavern of my heart, he helped me discern whether the formations I saw were unique or noteworthy…and whether I was even looking at them accurately. At one point, he shared his own struggles with anxiety. I found comfort in his story, mainly because he exuded the polar opposite of a stressed life. I discovered that his solace came through his own fires of anxiety.

Taking a hard look inside your heart is sort of like pulling the cushions off your sofa. You don't do it often but, when you do, you are always surprised by what you find. Missing things. Forgotten things. Gross things. In my house, you often find missing game pieces, one of the remotes, a few Legos, action figures, dust, some dead bugs, and a few dried up Cheerios. While you are somewhat embarrassed by what you find, you also enjoy the discovery.

That is what I felt like for those first few months.

Next, I talked with our elder board, the leaders of the church. They obviously needed to know what was going on. Again the response was favorable. I will never forget one elder telling me, "Next time, go ahead and faint. It's not a big deal." I think it was helpful advice, but I was not too sure I wanted to make a habit of fainting in front of a congregation of people. Maybe in some churches it would work to "liven up" the service…like being regularly "slain in the Spirit"…but in a Bible church, it simply would not have the same effect.

I also saw a doctor. In a passing comment, my dad once mentioned that our family had a history of atrial fibrillation. He called it a "fluttering heart." Without warning, your heart can start beating excessively fast. The resulting anxiety can trigger a vicious cycle. It was a possible contributing factor to my own experience. I wore a heart monitor for a few days but nothing showed up. The only thing the full physical revealed was that I was borderline hypoglycemic. My body chews up sugar in a matter of minutes. Skip a meal and I can get light-headed, headaches, and even mild hand tremors. Add a dose of stress and a lack of appetite, and my blood sugar can do strange things to my body.

It provided another piece to the puzzle.

Getting things out in the open. Experiencing understanding and grace. Learning more about my body. All of it helped tremendously. Transport me into another church with another response and I might have been a ministerial casualty. Time to get another job. Sell insurance. Work retail. But the space and grace afforded me allowed me time to dig deeper, explore further.

Then, one day, I stumbled upon the story of Jacob.

I grew up in a church. Not a very good one but at least one which taught me the basic Bible stories. I knew of Jacob. As a fairly disciplined Christian, I had also read Genesis quite a number of times. But this time the story of Jacob caught my eye in a different way. I began to relate. I began to see myself in him. I began to understand his story differently.

Who is Jacob? What do you think about when you hear his name?

Ask a group of church outsiders those two questions and you may get some blank stares. The name is familiar but not that common. Some may have an inkling of the stories of Jacob and Esau in the Bible.

Ask people inside the church and the common answers I have heard are the following…

Isaac's son. Esau's brother. Momma's boy. Deceiver of his dad. Loved his wife Rachel, disliked his other wife Leah. Father of lots of kids. Angel wrestler.

Not much positive. Few mention Jacob as their spiritual hero. He is not an Abraham, a Moses, a David, a Daniel. No one says "dare to be a Jacob." We are generally more embarrassed by his life than inspired by it.

Yet scan the Bible and you find that Jacob is a major player.

Jacob is mentioned in 355 verses of the Bible, from the book of Genesis to the epistle of Hebrews. His story occupies the last twenty-five chapters of Genesis, half the book. More time is spent on the story of Jacob than on the stories of Abraham and Isaac combined.

In Chapter 32 of Genesis, Jacob's name is changed to "Israel." Thus for the rest of Scripture and really for all eternity, God's people are associated with the person of Jacob. The twelve gates of the eternal heavenly city of Jerusalem are inscribed *with the names of the twelve tribes of the children of Israel* (Rev. 21:12).

On twelve occasions in Scripture, God is called the "God of Abraham, Isaac, and Jacob/Israel" (Exodus 3:6, 15, 16; 4:5; 1 Kings 18:36; 1 Chronicles 29:18; 2 Chronicles 30:6; Matthew 22:32; Mark 12:26; Luke 20:37; Acts 3:13; 7:32). God identifies Himself with Israel's three originating patriarchs.

Abraham begat Isaac.

Isaac begat Jacob.

Three generations…each receiving the blessing and promise of God.

But on twenty-four *separate* occasions in Scripture, God is specifically called the "God of Jacob," "the Mighty One of Jacob," "the Holy One of Jacob," "the King of Jacob," or "the Portion of Jacob" (NKJV).[1]

May the LORD answer you in the day of trouble;
*May the name of the **God of Jacob** defend you* (Psalm 20:1).

The LORD Almighty is with us;
*The **God of Jacob** is our fortress. Selah* (Psalm 46:7, 11).

As for me, I will declare this forever;
*I will sing praise to the **God of Jacob*** (Psalm 75:9).

Sing for joy to God our strength;
*Shout aloud to the **God of Jacob*** (Psalm 81:1).

Tremble, O earth, at the presence of the LORD,
*At the presence of the **God of Jacob**,*
Who turned the rock into a pool of water,
The flint into a fountain of waters (Psalm 114:7-8).

*Blessed is he whose help is the **God of Jacob**,*
Whose hope is in the LORD his God (Psalm 146:5).

Many people shall come and say,
"Come, and let us go up to the mountain of the LORD,
*To the house of the **God of Jacob**;*
He will teach us His ways,
And we shall walk in His paths."
For out of Zion shall go forth the law,
And the word of the LORD from Jerusalem (Isaiah 2:3; Micah 4:2).

---

[1] *God of Jacob*, 2 Sam. 23:1; Ps. 20:1; 46:7, 11; 75:9; 76:6; 81:1, 4; 84:8; 94:7; 114:7; 146:5; Isa. 2:3; Mic. 4:2; Acts 7:46. *Holy One of Jacob*, Isa. 29:23. *King of Jacob*, Isa. 41:21. *Mighty One of Jacob*, Gen. 49:24; Ps. 132:2, 5; Isa. 49:26; 60:16. *Portion of Jacob*, Jer. 10:16; 51:19.

"Jacob shall no more be ashamed,
No more shall his face grow pale.
For when he sees his children,
The work of My hands, in his midst,
They will sanctify my name;
*They will sanctify the **Holy One of Jacob***
And will stand in awe of the God of Israel" (Isaiah 29:22b-23).

"All flesh shall know
That I, the LORD, am your Savior,
*And your Redeemer, the **Mighty One of Jacob**"* (Isaiah 49:26b).

*The **Portion of Jacob** is not like them,*
For He is the Maker of all things,
And Israel is the tribe of His inheritance;
The LORD of hosts is His name (Jeremiah 10:16; 51:19).

God is unashamed, even desirous, to be called the "God of Jacob."

And if you add in the number of times that God is called the "God of Israel," the new name given to Jacob by God, then you increase the total by another 201 references.

Amazing.

He is the God of Abraham. The God of the "father of many nations." He is the God who keeps His promise even when it seems humanly impossible.

He is the God of Isaac. The God of "laughter." He is the God who delights in surprising us, catching us off guard, bringing us joy in unexpected ways.

And He is the God of Jacob. The God of "heel-catchers."[2] The God who loves us despite ourselves, who never gives up on us, who catches us even when we are desperately pursuing other things.

Quite simply…if God can love Jacob, then He can love anyone.

Even you.

Even me.

Especially you.

Especially me.

In 2006, I was drawn to Jacob's well. I drank in Jacob's story. And I was refreshed by the God who created him, chose him, pursued him, loved him.

And that well continues to sustain me today.

---

[2] "Jacob" comes from the Hebrew, *Ya`aqob,* meaning "heel grabber" or "heel catcher." It was the name given to Jacob in light of his unusual birth in which he emerges from the womb holding onto the heel of his twin brother, Esau (cf. Gen. 25:26). "In the view of the parents, the seizing of the heel would have conveyed an affectionate thought. On later reflection they would realize that the child was in essence struggling for the best starting position" (Ross, *Creation & Blessing,* p. 441).

CHAPTER THREE
A DAD NAMED LAUGHTER
Genesis 21-25

G od's Word is *living and active*.[3] It breathes. It speaks. It has a pulse. It is not magical or mystical. It is Spirit-ual. When we approach the Bible with humility and vulnerability, the Spirit of God operates on our hearts.

That means that the stories in Genesis are not just ancient myths about dead guys in the Middle East. Yes, there are cultural differences. Figuring out customs, geography, timelines, language, laws, and literary context takes work. God doesn't always put His treasures on the bottom shelf. He wants to see how serious we are. If you are looking for a quick mantra or secret formula to solve all your problems, look elsewhere. If you are looking for a strenuous transformation from the inside out, dig into God's Word.

Like a mirror, the Bible reflects our lives back to us.[4] The stories of Scripture become our own. Though we are separated by time and space from the people of the Bible, we bear the same image of God. We share the same struggle with sin. They are our fellow travelers on the journey.

We walk the same earth.

We breathe the same air.

---

[3] Hebrews 4:12, *For the word of God is living and active and sharper than any two-edged sword, and piercing as far as the division of soul and spirit, of both joints and marrow, and able to judge the thoughts and intentions of the heart.* (NASB)

[4] James 1:23-24, *For if anyone is a hearer of the word and not a doer, he is like a man who looks intently at his natural face in a mirror. For he looks at himself and goes away and at once forgets what he was like.* (ESV)

We drink the same water.

We relate to the same God.

I used to read Jacob's story as an interesting biblical biography. Check it off my Read-the-Bible-in-One-Year list. Try to cull a few nice lessons for my life. Shake my head at the strange world in which they lived.

Now instead of seeing the strangeness, I see the similarity.

The eternal Author of Scripture spans the gap of time to connect my life with the lives of those who have gone before.

God used the story of Jacob to speak to my own.

But before getting to know Jacob, let's take a look at his father.

Of the three patriarchs—Abraham, Isaac, and Jacob—Isaac is the "quiet one." The middle child of the patriarchs. So little is known about him.

We know about Abraham. God called him out of a pagan land in Genesis 12. Abram (as he was known then) obeyed. God promised to make him a great nation, to bless him, and to make his name great. God also promised to make his life a blessing to others.

Now the LORD said to Abram,
"Go from your country and your kindred and your father's house
to the land that I will show you.
And I will make of you a great nation,
and I will bless you and make your name great,
so that you will be a blessing.
I will bless those who bless you,
and him who dishonors you I will curse,
and in you all the families of the earth shall be blessed" (12:1-3).

Abram departed his homeland with his wife, Sarai. They had no children…though they brought along their nephew, Lot. The journey was not easy, and the promise did not come quickly.

For the next twenty-five years, Abram and Sarai waited for a child of their own. They wondered if they misheard God or whether God really understood the whole pregnancy process. They even tried to help God out with the promise. Abram, at the urging of Sarai, slept with one of Sarai's servant girls in order to produce an heir.

A child was born.

Ishmael.

But he was not the son that God intended…nor the son that Sarai wanted.

Along the way we learn about the person of Abraham. His faith in God. His humility and graciousness with Lot. His bravery in battle. His love and sensitivity toward Sarai. His incessant fear of being harmed by other men because of Sarai's remarkable beauty.

Abraham loved God and he loved his wife.

He was not a perfect man but a man always progressing in his walk with God.

Finally, after twenty-five years of waiting, Abraham and Sarah (as she was later called) gave birth to Isaac. His name means "laughter."

Abraham was close to 100 years old—Sarah close to 90—when they received word from God that a baby was on the way.

Abraham laughed with disbelief. "Is it even possible, Lord? Why can't You just be satisfied with Ishmael?"[5]

Sarah laughed in cynicism. "Yeah, right. We can't even enjoy sex much less get pregnant."[6]

But the pregnancy came about.

They both laughed with wondrous, almost silly, joy when Isaac actually arrived.

Sarah could barely contain herself. *"God has made me laugh, so that all who hear will laugh with me"* (Genesis 21:6).

It was too good to be true.

A worn-out, wrinkled woman nursing a newborn.

A broken-hearted, barren woman staring into the eyes of her newborn named "Laughter."

Isaac's birth was a miracle but, biblically-speaking, much of his life is a mystery.

We know he was loved. Showered with love. After waiting twenty-five plus years for a child, Abraham and Sarah were not going to short-change the experience. We can only imagine that Laughter grew up with lots of laughter around him. Every day was a party. The little child was doted upon, stared at, cuddled, held, hugged, kissed, loved.

Isaac was so loved that God ultimately had to test the heart of Abraham (Genesis 22).

---

[5] Genesis 17:17-18, *Then Abraham fell on his face and laughed, and said in his heart, "Shall a child be born to a man who is one hundred years old? And shall Sarah, who is ninety years old, bear a child?" And Abraham said to God, "Oh, that Ishmael might live before You!"*
[6] Genesis 18:11-12, *Abraham and Sarah were already very old, and Sarah was past the age of childbearing. So Sarah laughed to herself as she thought, "After I am worn out and my lord is old, will I now have this pleasure?"*

"Do you still love Me more than your son, your only son, the son whom you love?"

God asked for the sacrifice of Isaac. Abraham obeyed. Isaac complied. And God provided a substitute at the last moment.

The next scene in the Bible is Sarah's death, some twenty years later, followed immediately by a search for a wife for Isaac.

One gets the impression that Isaac was so attached to his mother, and vice-versa, that no other woman would have had a chance at the affections of his heart while she still lived. The biblical mandate for a man to *leave his father and mother and be joined to his wife* (2:24) would not have come easily to Isaac...nor to Sarah.

Indeed, when a wife is found, a beautiful young woman by the name of Rebekah, the Bible notes, *Then Isaac brought her into his mother Sarah's tent; and he took Rebekah and she became his wife, and he loved her. So Isaac was comforted after his mother's death* (24:67).

Freud would have a field day with such a verse. But no complex psychoanalysis is needed.

For thirty-seven years, Isaac experienced family life in a triad—Abraham, Sarah, and himself. He was by all accounts an only child. Ishmael had long departed the scene. Travel was limited. Neighbors were few. Extended relatives were far away. Meals, work, play were all shared together in this little family.

Isaac knew no other life.

The death of Sarah hit hard. Abraham mourned and wept for the loss of his lifelong companion. The Bible records the great pains he went through to bury her properly (Genesis 23).

Interestingly Isaac does not even enter the biblical narrative. He remains hidden in the background. We can only surmise that he grieved silently, on his own.

This was new territory for Isaac. Uncharted waters. The triad he had known all his life was down to two.

The young man named Laughter learned to cry.

It is in this atmosphere that Abraham commissioned one of his trusted servants to find a wife for Isaac (Genesis 24). Not just any wife but a wife from Abraham and Sarah's homeland, from their people, from their blood. A journey that takes the servant several months and several hundred miles providentially nets a young woman named Rebekah, Abraham's great niece.

To her credit (or perhaps some will say to her naiveté), Rebekah trusts Abraham's servant and agrees to marry a man she has never seen in an unknown land 500 miles from home. Granted, she knows he is a wealthy man from a good family—for many women that's a good start—but everything else is a leap of faith.

Isaac and Rebekah first see each other from a distance. The narrative says that Isaac *went out to the field one evening to meditate* (24:63).

Here is a reflective man, possibly an introvert, clearing his mind, conversing with God, contemplating companionship.

In the twilight, on the horizon, a caravan appears.

The silhouette of a woman catches his eye.

A bride has been found.

Introductions are brief.

Courtship takes place in a matter of minutes.

The marriage is consummated that evening.

And he took Rebekah and she became his wife, and he loved her. So Isaac was comforted after his mother's death (24:67).

Much of what we can discern about young Isaac is found in this verse.

He loved her.

Isaac was a sensitive man, a man deeply capable of love. Within a day, Isaac's heart was bonded to Rebekah. There were no barriers to intimacy in his heart. He had no bitterness. No walls. No scars. No baggage. He had bathed in the love of both of his parents. Love came easily to him. What he had freely received all of his life, he was freely able to give.

So Isaac was comforted after his mother's death.

Isaac's love for Rebekah restored joy to his heart.

He was able to laugh again…even in the midst of his grief.

From all indications, Isaac and Rebekah developed a healthy, intimate marriage. Of course, an early blot on his record occurs in Genesis 26. Isaac, like his father, fears for his life because of the beauty of his wife. In that culture, having a gorgeous wife can get you killed.

The 70's song "When You're in Love with a Beautiful Woman" could certainly be sung by both Abraham and Isaac.

When you're in love with a beautiful woman, it's hard
When you're in love with a beautiful woman, you know it's hard
Everybody wants her, everybody loves her
Everybody wants to take your baby home[7]

Isaac is asked about Rebekah by some men in the city. Obviously her skin, hair, figure, and smile diverted a number of male eyes toward her.

Out of fear, Isaac says that she is his sister.

Here is the logic. A man may harm a husband to get a woman he desperately wants. But he will befriend a brother to get to his sister.

---

[7] Evan Stevens, songwriter, 1978. Performed by Dr. Hook & the Medicine Show.

Isaac plays things safe even if it does potentially expose his wife to unwanted advances.

It is easy to fault Isaac…as well as Abraham before him…for such a spineless decision. There is no excuse for their deceit or their cowardice. But the recurrence of the incident in the Genesis narrative tells us that the threat is real. Isaac and Abraham are herders and shepherds not warriors and soldiers. Though Abraham does get his feet wet in battle (Genesis 14), Isaac goes to great lengths to avoid conflict and confrontation (Genesis 26). Isaac can't be excused but he can be understood. His deception doesn't reveal a lack of love for Rebekah but rather a lack of courage on his own part.

To prove the point, the ruse is discovered when Isaac is seen *showing endearment* to Rebekah in a public place (26:8). The Hebrew word can be translated as "laughing, playing, or toying" with someone else.

Ironically, it is the same root as Isaac's name.[8]

Laughter is laughing with, playing with, toying with Rebekah. His hands are all over her, tickling her, fondling her, enjoying her.

And it is apparent that this is not a normal brother-sister relationship.

Though the chronology of Genesis 26 is unclear, the impression is that Isaac and Rebekah are still goofy, playful, romantic "lovebirds" after many years of marriage.

Isaac's prayer for Rebekah further exemplifies his love (25:21). Like Sarah, Rebekah is barren. Twenty years pass in their marriage with no missed period, no pregnancy, no child.

My wife and I struggled for four years with infertility. Not a long time in the grand scheme of things but enough time to taste the disappointment and ride

---

[8] Hebrew, *taschaq*, "to laugh, mock, play," blueletterbible.org.

the emotional roller coaster of infertility. Every month is another chance, another ray of hope, another possibility. But at the very time when a woman's emotions are the most tender, the heartache hits. Month after month, year after year, the ups and downs and the sharp turns of the emotional roller coaster continue.

Forty-eight months was enough of a struggle for my wife and myself. I can't even imagine 240 months.

Laughter prays.

Laughter loves.

Laughter cries.

Laughter pleads.

And God answers his prayer.

Twins are soon discovered in Rebekah's womb.

All their hopes, dreams, and prayers will soon be answered.

They will become parents of two very different boys.

And their doting love for each other will face its greatest test and greatest stress.

STEVE FOSTER

CHAPTER FOUR
THE TWINS: HARRY & JAKE
Genesis 25:19-28

I was a sophomore in Bible college when the 1988 movie, *Twins,* came out. It starred two of the most diverse male actors in Hollywood, Arnold Schwarzenegger and Danny DeVito. If you looked at these two men side by side—Schwarzenegger with his tall, muscular, chiseled body and DeVito with his short, balding, squatty frame—you would never peg them as twins. Yet that was the premise of the movie.

Somehow, in a governmental experiment of genetic engineering, Schwarzenegger's character inherited all the premium genes while DeVito's character was conceived with all the junky genetic leftovers. They developed into two widely divergent individuals until one day they shockingly discovered that they were twins.

It was a crazy idea…that made a humorous movie…primarily because of how absurd such polar opposite twins could be.

But surprisingly, Genesis 25 is not too far from the same storyline.

Rebekah deals with infertility for twenty years. An eternity for a woman longing to be a mother. Her loving husband, Laughter (Isaac), prays fervently for her.

And miraculously…finally…joyfully…Rebekah becomes pregnant.

As her belly expands, however, her fears expand as well.

It feels like a war is going on in her womb.

In an age before sonograms, Rebekah has no idea what is going on. For all she knows, she has a big baby bashing against her stomach wanting to come out, fighting against her, inside her.

Doubling over in pain at times when the internal fetal smashing strikes, she can barely breathe out a question, "If all is well, why this?" (25:22).

In pain and confusion, she inquires of the LORD…perhaps even consulting her father-in-law, Abraham, for his intercession and insight.

A divine answer arrives.

Two nations are in your womb.
Two peoples shall be separated from your body.
One people shall be stronger than the other,
And the older shall serve the younger. (25:23)

TWINS!

A double blessing.

They prayed for a child and received two by surprise.

But these two would be anything but identical.

They wouldn't even be congenial.

They would be as different as night and day and as agreeable as two starving teenage boys fighting over the last slice of pizza.

The birth itself would be memorable as well.

The first baby comes out beet red…with hair all over his body. Possibly a condition called lanugo which affects some preemies. Holding their newborn baby, the affectionate name Esau (hairy) immediately comes to mind.

As if delivering a red fur baby wasn't surprising enough, the second baby is born holding onto his older brother Harry's heel…as if trying to hold him back from emerging first.

Endearingly, they call him Jacob.

"Heelcatcher."

Genesis 25:27-28 pack a semi-truck trailer full of personality differences, masculinity issues, and family dynamics into twenty-two Hebrew words.

So the boys grew.
And Esau was a skillful hunter, a man of the field;
But Jacob was a mild man, dwelling in tents.
And Isaac loved Esau because he ate of his game,
But Rebekah loved Jacob.

Two boys. Twins. Born at the same time from the same womb.

Worlds apart.

Harry was a "man's man."

In today's world, he would have a long beard like the dudes on *Duck Dynasty*. Cowboy hat. Jeans. Boots. Leather belt with a Texas belt buckle. Big ol' truck. Mud on the tires. Gun rack in the back. Deer strapped to the hood. NRA sticker proudly plastered on the back window. A bumper sticker loudly proclaiming, "Keep Honking. I'm Reloading."

Jake, on the other hand, was a "momma's boy."

In today's world, he would have the clean face. Plastic rim glasses. Button up shirt. Dockers pants. Dress shoes. Degrees on the wall. Books on the shelf. Ipad in hand. He drives a gas-saving Toyota Prius to the office. No bumper stickers. Just a perfectly placed logo identifying the subdivision he lives in.

The hunter and the reader.

The outdoorsman and the "indoorsman."

The jock and the nerd.

The stud and the student.

Amazingly, the Bible presents them not only as twin brothers but also as two very different versions of masculinity.

A number of years ago, John Eldredge wrote a book entitled, *Wild at Heart.*[9] It was a clarion call for men "to be men." To be adventurous. To be daring. To step out and be leaders. It was a prophetic message against the passivity of men and the feminization of the church.

My older brother read it and absolutely loved it.

I read it and felt like the book was missing something.

Let me explain…

I am the youngest of six children…with two older brothers.

My older brothers could be classified as "Esau men."

My oldest brother, Scott, was a phenomenal athlete. The one all the coaches wanted for their Little League baseball team. Strong. Coordinated. Determined. A first-class golfer…the sport my dad played and loved. Taking our little Florida high school to two state championships. Sinking two hole-in-ones in his sophomore year. Getting an opportunity to play golf for the University of Florida…but wasting it in pursuit of drugs.

My other brother, Rob, was a body builder. Chiseled arms. Tan skin. Strong muscles. Driving a tan muscle car, a souped-up Mustang. Driving fast. Living large. Attracting the girls. Working hard. Building a deck for my dad in the backyard. Becoming an Iron Man competitor later in life. Swimming 2.4 miles,

---

[9] John Eldredge, *Wild at Heart* (Nashville, TN: Thomas Nelson, 2001).

biking 112 miles, then running a marathon. In the same day! Still competing into his mid-50's.

And then there's me.

I probably haven't swum 2.4 miles, biked 112 miles, and run 26 miles…in my lifetime!

As a child, I preferred to stay inside. Read. Study. Be creative. Write. Draw. Invent new games. Race Matchbox cars through our house and keep stats on each of the races.

I got straight A's from first grade until my doctorate degree.

The honor student. The geek. The nerd.

I didn't want to run and jump off a cliff. I preferred the stable and safe ground several feet away from the edge…with a nice guardrail and clearly marked signs warning of danger.

With apologies to John Eldredge…I was "mild at heart."

Not being an "Esau man" like my brothers, I struggled with my own masculinity.

What does it mean to be a man?

I think every boy asks that question at some point in his life.

Some find that they fit the cultural mold rather early in life. They develop facial hair in the sixth grade, grow strong, succeed in sports, love the outdoors, shoot guns, take risks, buy big trucks.

Others are drawn to music, to the arts, to academics. Masculinity is often an elusive concept for them. Unfortunately, in trying to fire up men "to be men," we often reinforce cultural stereotypes that lead many mild-mannered men to doubt who they are.

The Bible highlights two very different men…from the same womb…born at the same time…to signal that the spectrum of masculinity (and femininity for that matter) is much broader than we often portray.

Both Esau and Jacob are men. Both are masculine. Both express strength…but in different ways. There is not only strength of the body…but also strength of mind, strength of artistry, strength of compassion, strength of self-control, strength of character.

Our culture's inability…and even the church's inability…to grasp this concept has unwittingly fed into the gender confusion and superficial stereotypes that plague our media, our society, and, unfortunately, many individual men today.

In the case of Esau and Jacob, the confusion was further fed by the responses of the parents. Isaac loved Esau and Rebekah loved Jacob.

The differences of the twins led to a division in the family.

Up until this point, Isaac and Rebekah appear to be two godly individuals who love each other and love the Lord. But the pressures and stresses of raising two rambunctious, incompatible boys expose some cracks in their individual lives and in their marriage.

The pressures of life reveal the flaws in our lives.

We often blame the pressures. We hate our circumstances. We think, "If only I didn't have this problem in my life, then I would be fine."

But the reality is that the flaws are already there. Pressure only exposes them.

Isaac has a serious flaw in his character.

James Montgomery Boice notes, "Isaac loved Esau more than Jacob because he had a taste for the wild game Esau caught and probably also because he possessed characteristics and abilities lacking in himself."[10]

Deep down, Isaac was probably more like Jacob than Esau. Quiet. Conflict-averse. Doted on by his father and mother. Pampered. Insecure.

Perhaps Isaac lived out some of his dreams through the wild, aggressive, carefree nature of his oldest son.

Whatever the case, Isaac definitely loved to eat meat.

And Esau was the reliable source of freshly killed, finely seasoned venison.

Isaac went from a man with a tender heart to a man with a tenacious palate. He went from being a spiritual man, meditating and praying, to being a "carnal" man, marinating and fileting. He went from being hungry for God to being hungry for a plate of deer sausage.

Why? What changed?

Perhaps the change came slowly, almost unnoticeably. Often spiritual decline is a gradual slope. But one significant event did happen while Esau and Jacob were teenagers…Abraham died.

If you look at the biblical chronology, Abraham has Isaac when he is 100 years old, Isaac has Jacob and Esau when he is 60, and then Abraham dies when he is 175.[11] So Abraham dies when the twins are 15 years old. Isaac seems to start losing a bit of his spiritual fervor once Abraham dies.

Sometimes our faith is so dependent on the strength of someone else's that we begin to falter when they are gone. The spiritually strong wife supports the faith of her husband…then she dies and his tottering faith begins to crumble. Or the

---

[10] James Montgomery Boice, *Genesis*, vol. 2 (Grand Rapids, MI: Baker Books, 1998), p. 738.
[11] Genesis 21:5; 25:7; 25:26.

obedient child thrives spiritually while he is at home…but then heads off to college and finds that his personal faith is undeveloped and easily distracted or destroyed.

Isaac was so loved by Abraham and Sarah that when they both passed away, he seems unprepared to live the life of faith alone. The cracks in his spiritual foundation are revealed.

Isaac and Rebekah's marriage also suffers. They don't necessarily stop loving each other…they just start loving other things more. Isaac starts loving his redneck son, Esau, and his steak dinners. Rebekah starts loving her sensitive son, Jacob, and his help and companionship around the home.

And their drifting relationship from each other widens the rift in their family. Favorites are picked. Sides are formed. Resentment builds. Manipulation and deceit infect communication.

Studies have shown that picking favorites in the family is not uncommon. In fact, estimates are that one-third to two-thirds of families have "parental favoritism." [12]

Parents tend to favor firstborn or lastborn children, since at some point they are the only children in the home. Firstborns generally get greater attention while lastborns get greater affection.

But regardless of the situation, the results are never pretty.

Disfavored children can act out in aggressiveness and rebellion or suffer from depression and low self-confidence.

Favored children, while reaping the benefits of parental attention, often feel the resentment of their siblings…and can become damaged emotionally by a parent who leans on them or confides in them as a de facto spouse.

---

[12] Ilan Shrira, "When Parents Play Favorites," *Psychology Today,* January 9, 2009.

In my own family, I was often humorously…and probably at times resentfully…called "mom's favorite." I was the child born in her later years. The unplanned surprise. Born almost six years after my nearest sibling.

From what I have been told, my mom was on the birth control pill. They were finished with having children. Five was enough. But while on the pill, she developed fibroid tumors. The doctor told her to stop taking the pill for a while to see if they would clear up. When she asked about the possibility of getting pregnant, the doctor assured her that it would take a few weeks before her fertility would return. However, to her surprise, at her next doctor's appointment, she didn't have any fibroid tumors but she did have a sixth pregnancy.

Me.

The little fibroid tumor baby.

Growing up, I always felt loved by my mother. But, at the same time, I often felt unwanted by my father and somewhat isolated from my older siblings. They were a unit unto themselves, five children born within seven years of each other, and I was the addendum, the appendix.

Family dynamics are a field of study unto themselves but one thing is for sure…we are impacted by our home environment, especially by our attachments, or lack of attachments, to our mom and to our dad.

I am realizing this more and more.

Jacob experienced it in his family about four thousand years ago.

Cultures change…but human nature remains the same.

The "heelcatcher" was attached to his mom, detached from his dad, and vastly different from his twin brother.

He experienced love but longed for more. After all, almost every boy can count on the love of a mom…the deeper desire is for the affirmation and blessing of a dad. This desire is only amplified when another sibling seems to have it and you don't.

Jacob was a man struggling to know who he was.

He was a man uncomfortable in his own skin.

So eventually…like many of us…he would find himself trying on the skin of someone else…anyone else…as long as it promised a drop of affirmation to his thirsty soul.

CHAPTER FIVE
THE ART OF HEELCATCHING
Genesis 25:29-34

I have four boys.

They are vastly different but they share one thing in common…they are extremely competitive. When they were growing up, practically everything in our household became a competition. Who could race up the stairs first? Who could finish their meal first? Who could run fastest? Who could throw furthest? Who could burp loudest?

One thing I have learned in raising four boys is that the hunger for strength and competence resides deep in a boy's heart. The key question I think every boy asks himself is, "Am I strong?"

When my boys were young, strength was measured in muscles.

"Dad, check out my muscles," as they flexed the biggest bicep they could pop up.

"Dad, look at my six-pack," as they did their best to tighten their stomach muscles. What they thought was a "six-pack" was generally just four skinny ribs and a slightly developed abdominal muscle underneath.

As boys get older, strength is measured in competence. What am I good at? Do I measure up? And how do I compare to others?

This is where competition comes into play. How do I stack up compared to others? The only way you know you are good at baseball is to be better than everyone else in your age bracket. To crown a winner in a competition means that there has to be a whole host of losers.

Some young men find a source of competence early in life. They find that they are good at baseball, basketball, football, taekwondo, music, math, golf. They succeed until, inevitably, they come up against those who are better than themselves or they find that the peak of "victory mountain" is often a lonely, unsatisfying place to be…and usually very short-lived.

Meanwhile many other young men wander aimlessly from place to place, activity to activity, trying to find competence in illusionary things (e.g., video games and fantasy), exerting their strength in illegitimate ways (e.g., anger, rebellion, violence), or giving up on the whole affair and becoming passive, addictive, or self-indulgent.

But the desire for strength remains…whether it is amplified or anesthetized.

"Heelcatching" is just one strategy in this quest for strength, for competence, for competition.

Jacob received the name "heelcatcher" innocently enough. He was born with a hand clutching onto his brother's ankle. It looked like a desire to be close. It was actually a desire to get ahead.

Somehow as the twins smashed against each other in the womb, Esau found himself at the lower part of the birth canal when contractions began. He was "in the right place at the right time"…fortunately…sovereignly…positioned to emerge first.

Even as an in utero baby, Jacob was not happy with this arrangement. His infantile intuition was already imprinted with an impulse to be first. Almost as if trying to pull his brother back in the womb, his hand snatched at his twin brother's heel. But his secondary position was predetermined and his strength was too weak to change things.

Not until later in life would he learn...probably in the quiet hours before bedtime as his mother tucked him in...that God had already revealed in a mysterious pre-birth oracle that *the older would serve the younger* (25:23).

Jacob held onto this thought...even while this little secret tidbit was probably held away from Esau.

As the two boys developed into very different teenagers...Esau becoming the all-state quarterback in high school...Jacob recording the stats on the sideline...the "heelcatcher" plotted his next move.

The art of heelcatching involves finding a way, regardless of the means, to get ahead of anyone standing in your way...or anyone who happens to be in the same race you are.

The picture that comes to mind is of two football players running after a loose ball. As one gets closer to the ball, the other yanks his heel to trip him up...at the same time, propelling himself forward to grab the ball first.

In football it is one thing...in life it is another.

The heelcatcher may be the person who cheats to get good grades, who lies to get what he wants, who takes shortcuts to gain an advantage, who angles for the promotion...or he may be more like the person who drives himself to succeed, studying harder, working longer, becoming perfectionistic, ambitious, relentless, to make sure that in the game of life, he is better or more competent than someone else...everyone else.

The competitions of our childhood don't end in puberty...they just become more sophisticated.

Jacob, as his name implies, had mastered the art of heelcatching.

And his brother, the good ol' boy with the eye for tracking and trapping deer, had no clue that he was about to be schooled by a better hunter.

The selling of the birthright in Genesis 25:29-34 seems like such a strange story in our day and age. A weird kind of transaction for a weird kind of privilege. Why in the world would the Bible pause its redemptive narrative to tell us such an obscure event in Esau and Jacob's life?

Because the biblical narrative, particularly in Genesis, is centered on a promise. A divine promise given to Abraham, passed down to Isaac, alluded to in the birth of Esau and Jacob.

"I will make you a great nation;
I will bless you
And make your name great;
And you shall be a blessing.
I will bless those who bless you,
And I will curse him who curses you;
And in you all the families of the earth shall be blessed." (12:2-3).

How much Jacob understands or even cares about this promise is not known at this point, but he at least knows that he is to be first…though he emerged from the womb second. He at least envisions that he is destined for greatness in comparison to his brother.

Deep down, he despises his cool but uncouth brother and strategizes a way to get ahead.

He sets a trap…using food as his bait.

Cooking a savory stew, he lets the aroma waft through the tent.

Esau, coming in from a long day in the field, without a kill, is tired, frustrated, and hungry. The perfect combination for poor decision-making.

Esau smells the stew and barges into the kitchen, basically grunting out in hunger.

"Give me some of that red stuff! Red stuff! I need it now! I am starving and exhausted!" (25:30).

Jacob makes his move.

"First sell me your birthright" (25:31).

What a strange exchange. I'll give you a bowl of soup for the right to be called the firstborn.

What a conniving brother!

Again, we can't quite fathom the moment.

Perhaps a comparison in our world would be a brother making fresh chocolate chip cookies, hot out of the oven, letting the aroma drift through the house, as his dessert-loving older brother comes back from a long day of football practice.

"Hey, bro, give me some of those cookies! Whoa, chocolate chip cookies! I am so hungry and they smell so good!"

"Sure, bro, but remember those future stock options that Dad put in your name when you were young? Transfer those over to me and you can have all the cookies you want."

"Stock options?! I have no idea what those things are anyway. Sure. Just give me those cookies!"

It is such a foolish exchange…and such an out-of-context request…that it almost seems like a joke.

Surely he isn't serious?

Jacob, however, is deadly serious.

"Swear to me as of this day" (25:33).

Esau…convinced he is starving…flippant about the future…takes an oath.

"Whatever, bro. With God as my witness, the birthright is yours."

Jacob seals the deal, gives the stew to his brother, and even throws in a side of freshly baked biscuits to make Esau feel like he made a wise choice.

Esau slurps it down, gulps a big glass of water, gets up, and goes his way.

And the Bible says, *Thus Esau despised his birthright* (25:34).

It is a clarifying moment.

Esau is revealed as a *profane man.*[13] A thoughtless man. A godless man. A fool. A man hungry for immediate gratification regardless of the consequences.

The "birthright" represented all the Middle Eastern rights of the firstborn, the privileged position of the family, the representative of the father, the double portion of the inheritance, and, in this case, the recipient of the divine promise and blessing.

These things mean nothing to Esau. "Just give me my Bud, my burger, my shotgun, my LazyBoy, and my flat screen, and I am happy. Who cares about retirement, stock options, and inheriting the family business?"

Jacob, on the other hand, is a master at the game.

He is like the chess player that purposely exposes a pawn so that his impatient, careless, novice opponent takes the bait and exposes his king.

Checkmate.

Esau is too easy of a target for a "heelcatcher" like Jacob.

Esau despises his birthright. He is a foolish man.

And Jacob despises his brother. He is a selfish man.

---

[13] Hebrews 12:16, *Lest there be any fornicator or profane person like Esau, who for one morsel of food sold his birthright* (NKJV).

The Bible tells this story with little commentary.

The reader is left hanging as the narrative moves on to Isaac passing off Rebekah as his sister to avoid danger and digging wells all over the desert to avoid conflict (Genesis 26).

But the die is cast.

Esau is a man who makes bad choices from a bad character while Jacob is a man who makes good choices…successful, strategic choices…but also from a bad character. At this point, Jacob is not any better than Esau…just a whole lot smarter.

Jacob succeeds…he gets ahead…he wins…but he is still empty.

Heelcatching works, but it does not satisfy.

When I entered fifth grade, I was assigned to Mrs. Thompson's class. Mrs. Thompson had the reputation of being a mean, crusty, old-school teacher. I was nervous but determined to be one of the few people to excel in her class.

One of the subjects in fifth grade was the history of civilizations. The final grade was determined by ten tests throughout the year. I made a "zero" on the first test. A zero! I answered all the questions correctly…but I forgot to put my name on the test. A big Mrs. Thompson "no no." She gave me a zero on a test that I had aced. I was livid. I appealed. I begged. To no avail. The crusty old teacher was calcified in her crusty old rules.

I was devastated.

But I made a resolution. I would not miss another question on another history of civilizations test. Nine 100's would be the only way to counteract the one "0" and still give me the lowest possible "A" in the subject.

I literally memorized the chapters to make sure that no question surprised me or hindered my quest for perfection.

And I did it. Nine 100's for the rest of the semester. An "A" in the subject...at the expense of peace of mind, rest, and the general enjoyment of life in the fifth grade.

What was driving my ten-year old mind? Why in the world was an "A" in one subject in fifth grade the holy grail?

In the summer before fifth grade, I watched my older sister, Jan, graduate as valedictorian. Top in her class. Decked in gold. Honored before her classmates. Giving a graduation speech as the mark of her achievements. It became my goal to follow in her footsteps.

I guess I didn't realize that fifth grade scores didn't count toward high school GPA.

Or maybe I didn't care.

If I couldn't compete in sports or physical strength like my brothers, then I would compete in academics. I would best them. I would best others. I would find affirmation in the gold-decked honors of straight "A's," tassels, degrees, accolades, and recognition from others.

Summa cum laude.

Above others in distinction.

But still starving in the soul.

If your goal is simply to be better than the next guy...to be smarter...to be wealthier...to be more successful...to have the bigger title...the bigger house...the nicer car...the nicer vacations...the more impressive Facebook page...then ultimately, eventually, it will backfire.

Esau was hungry for the wrong things and it made him a fool.

Ironically, Jacob was also a fool. He just didn't realize it yet.

We are all hungry for something. We are all driven by desire. We go after that which we think will satisfy our craving...make us happy...bring us delight...make us strong...make us significant.

The Esaus of the world try to satiate this hunger with cheap thrills, with immediate gratification, with whatever feels good at the time. They sell their future for momentary pleasure. They give up their birthright for a bowl of stew.

Meanwhile, the Jacobs of the world take a long-range approach. They see the goal in the future. They plot their strategy, get their education, make the sacrifices, pursue their dreams, do everything they can to succeed...regardless of who it hurts or what it costs. But, in the end, they are also chasing the wrong thing.

Like King Solomon discovered many generations after Jacob:

So I became great and surpassed all who were before me in Jerusalem.
Also my wisdom remained with me.
And whatever my eyes desired I did not keep from them.
I kept my heart from no pleasure,
for my heart found pleasure in all my toil,
and this was my reward for all my toil.
Then I considered all that my hands had done
and the toil I had expended in doing it,
and behold, all was vanity and a striving after wind,
and there was nothing to be gained under the sun (Ecclesiastes 2:9-11).

The deepest hunger we have will not be satisfied with temporal things.

And for a heelcatcher, it usually takes being tripped up and falling flat on your face before you finally figure it out.

CHAPTER SIX
THE HUNGER FOR BLESSING
Genesis 27

"Unwanted"

The word seemed to jump off the page.

I was at a marriage seminar with my wife, Liz. We were doing an exercise together, re-visiting a past argument and remembering the feelings that we had at the moment of our highest tension. A list of words acted as prompts for our memory.

Lonely. Dismissed. Unimportant. Helpless. Scared. Hopeless. Hurt. Intimidated. Threatened. Panicked. Rejected. Inadequate. Alone. Confused. Lost. Embarrassed. Ashamed. Isolated. Small. Insignificant. Unwanted. Afraid. Humiliated. Disappointed.

I would not have predicted that the word "unwanted" would touch a nerve in me. But it did.

I stopped and reflected.

In the midst of tension with my wife, during the times I feel the most disconnected from her, the feeling that often overwhelms me is the feeling of being unwanted.

Do you still want me?

A flood of memories rushed into my mind…like a dam had been released.

I remembered growing up as the youngest in my family. The unplanned surprise. The large gap of age between me and my next oldest brother. In many ways I was both a lastborn and an only child. By the time I was ten, I was practically the only one left in the home.

I felt loved by my mom, but I often wondered if I was wanted by my dad.

My "surprise" changed the family dynamic. Five children born within seven years of each other is enough of a dynamic in itself. My dad wasn't necessarily a "family man" to begin with. He left much of the parenting to my mom. She was a non-stop caretaker. A woman who would sacrifice everything for her family. She grew up the youngest of eleven. Poor. Neglected. Abused. She made a vow that none of her children would feel the same neglect.

My dad was a good man. A hard-working man. A man who believed that providing for his family was the highest good he could achieve…the best gift he could give. He worked late most evenings. Played golf whenever he could. Read the paper and watched the news and episodes of *HeeHaw* when he was home. He was physically present but emotionally absent.

My five older siblings were so close in age. A handful of kids, moving through the early stages of life together. The picture I remember the most in our hallway was a black and white picture of the five of them…dressed in Sunday clothes…my sisters with their light hair and tan skin…my oldest brother Scott with a crew cut and big toothy smile… my nearest brother Rob sitting in the front…about two years old…with a little boys' suit and a bow tie…the hands of his sisters on his shoulders…enveloping him…embracing him as the youngest.

I am not in the picture.

In fact, by the time I came along, the picture-taking apparently stopped.

Looking through old family photo albums, there are black and white pictures of all of my siblings as they grew up. The only evidence of my infant and toddler days are a few Polaroids, seemingly taken on the same day.

My brother Rob used to tell me I was hatched…or found in the woods by my parents. It was his way of aggravating his annoying little brother…and perhaps sub-consciously getting back at the one who disrupted the family and stole the coveted lastborn position from him.

One of the earliest memories I have in life goes back to when I was probably four years old. My dad worked at a large company called Johns-Manville in Green Cove Springs, Florida. In my little mind, it was the biggest building in the world. An immense box-like building with a square camel hump in the middle. The words "Johns-Manville" spelled in big white letters in the expansive, landscaped, grassy field in front.

My dad came home in the middle of the day looking for me. He said that he needed me at work. I thought, "Whoa, I'm going to that big building! My dad needs me!"

My dad had locked himself out of his office and no one had an extra key. His office was on the first floor on the outside wall. The windows opened at a slant, just wide enough for someone small to squeeze through. I can remember being lifted up on his shoulders, crawling through the window, standing on a large metal filing cabinet, and then stepping down onto a table and then onto the floor. I ran through the inside and opened his office door. Everyone in the office clapped for me and laughed with my dad.

The next thing I knew, I was back at home.

It was a short event…but a lasting memory.

I was needed. My dad needed me.

Up until this point in my life, I have lived approximately 18,600 days. A billion little events have happened in my life. And this is one of the earliest ones that I remember.

It is not the events that have happened in our lives that really matter. It is the events that we remember...the stories that we re-visit...the stories that we tell...that really shape us.

In that story, I felt needed...valuable...wanted. It is a precious memory... especially since I don't remember many more like it during my early childhood years.

As we arrive in Genesis 27, we encounter a story that many of us are familiar with. Isaac is old. He is practically blind. He wants to give a final fatherly blessing to his oldest son, Esau. But Jacob plays the deceiver...at the prompting of his mom...dresses up like Esau and steals the blessing.

It is another odd story with very little parallel in our current culture.

But the hungering for our father's blessing transcends all cultures.

We long to know that we are needed...valuable...wanted...especially by the one who fathered us.

Unfortunately, for Jacob, to get his father's blessing, he has to pretend that he is someone else.

Genesis 27 moves in five scenes with the third scene, the middle scene, serving as the heart of the story and its climax.

Scene One: Isaac's Darkness (27:1-4)

Isaac is old and blind, convinced that he is near death...even though Genesis will tell us that he will live for a few more decades after this.[14] Before he dies, he wants to bless Esau, his "older son," or more literally in Hebrew, his "greater son."

---

[14] After Jacob returns from a 20-year sojourn in Haran, Isaac is still alive and apparently he lives a few more years after Jacob's return (Genesis 35:27-29).

Isaac acts secretly. He is aware of the divine oracle that the *older would serve the younger* (25:23). But his love for Esau…and his love for eating wild game…cloud his vision. He is both physically blind and willfully blind. Unable to accept the prophecy of the divine oracle, unable to see the faults of his favorite son, unable to bear the thought of the smooth-skinned, tent-dwelling Jacob getting priority in the family.

The word "bless" is the key word in this story, used twenty-eight times, almost in every verse.[15]

It is a word that we are familiar with…after all, we use it every time someone sneezes. "God bless you!"

But its meaning is less clear in our minds.

One Hebrew dictionary perhaps captures its meaning best:

> God's blessing is his formative, empowering word, often with overtones of appointing destiny. *… That which is blessed functions and produces at the optimum level, fulfilling its divinely designated purpose* [emphasis added].
>
> …Nothing was more important than securing the blessing of God in one's life or nation. …Real success was impossible without the coveted blessing. "Where modern man talks of success, OT man talked of blessing" (Wenham).
>
> …It was taken for granted that there was an efficacy to blessings pronounced by certain individuals acting in harmony with the Lord (because of their authority, position, or special endowment). …Every father, tribal or national leader, king, or priest could potentially

---

[15] Genesis 27:4, 7, 10, 12, 19, 23, 25, 27, 29, 30, 31, 33, 34, 35, 36, 38, 41; 28:1, 3, 4, 6.

pronounce "inspired" words of empowerment, prayer, hope, benediction, or prophecy over his children or people.[16]

In summary, a blessing was a divinely-empowered, future-oriented affirmation pronounced over you...usually with the blesser's hands on your head...that identified your purpose in life and assured you of its fulfillment. A blessing told you who you were...why you were created...where you were headed. It answered all the questions of meaning that we struggle with in life. And pronounced by your father, it avowed your value, pointed you in the right direction, and freed you to be who you were created to be.

Isaac longed to give his blessing to Esau. Esau longed to receive it. But Rebekah had other ideas.

Scene Two: Rebekah's Determination (27:5-17)

Rebekah was listening when Isaac spoke to Esau (27:5). The verb, "listening," is the imperfect tense which implies that this was a regular habit of Rebekah. She functioned as the "ears" of the house and she seems to have anticipated that Isaac might try an end-around and give the blessing to Esau in stubborn contradiction to the word of the oracle.

From the day we first meet Rebekah in Scripture, she is a strong woman...a determined woman. Not many women have the gumption and the strength to draw water from a well...over and over again...to satiate the drinking capacity of a bunch of camels (24:19-20). So Rebekah is ready to act as soon as the opportunity demands it.

When Esau leaves to go hunting for his dad's favorite dinner, Rebekah springs to action. She finds Jacob and divulges her plan. She will cook the meal, skillfully

---

[16] Michael L. Brown, "Bless," *New International Dictionary of Old Testament Theology and Exegesis,* edited by Willem A. VanGemeren, (Grand Rapids, MI: Zondervan, 1997), pp. 757-767.

seasoning goat meat to taste like venison. Jacob will play the part of Esau, wearing goat skins to cover his smooth skin and to make it hairy like Harry's. And Isaac will play the goat, being fooled by his wife and his younger son.

Rebekah even has a choice set of Esau's clothes ready at her disposal (27:15). The Hebrew implies that she may have kept them in a special place to be used for such an occasion. This is not a haphazard plan. It has been formulated for a long time in the mind of the heelcatcher's mother.

Scene Three: Jacob's Disguise (27:18-29)

The climax of the scene occurs as Jacob dons Esau's clothes, attaches the goat skins to his smooth body, and carries Rebekah's finely prepared goat-venison meal into Isaac's presence.

The first question out of Isaac's mouth is *"Who are you, my son?"* (27:18).

Who…are…you?

Jacob answers this vital question with a lie.

"I am Esau, your firstborn" (27:19).

The voice has Jacob's ring to it but the blind Isaac isn't expecting a ruse.

He asks his son to come near and feels his hairy hands.

"Are you really my son Esau?" (27:24).

"I am" comes the reply.

Isaac wolfs down the deer-flavored goat meat…enjoys a glass of wine…wipes his mouth…rubs his full belly…and asks his son to come near for a kiss.

In many ways it is the kiss of betrayal.

The heelcatcher comes near to his father…perhaps as close as he has ever been… and gives him a kiss. This sign of affection…coupled with the distinct sweaty smell of Esau emitting from his clothes…confirms the deception.

Isaac pronounces his favored blessing on his "favored" son.

Ah, the smell of my son
Is like the smell of the field
That the LORD has blessed.
May God give you heaven's dew
And earth's richness
An abundance of grain and new wine.
May nations serve you
And peoples bow down to you.
Be lord over your brothers
And may the sons of your mother bow down to you.
May those who curse you be cursed
And those who bless you be blessed (27:27b-29).

Isaac's blessing on Esau…pronounced on Jacob.

As the words flowed from Isaac's mouth, Jacob must have reveled in their power…their poetry…their passion. These were words that Jacob probably longed to hear from his father. He longed to be affirmed…to be loved…to be blessed by his father.

Now he was…but only disguised as Esau.

Jacob had to pretend to be someone else to be blessed.

He had to wear a mask.

He had to don goat skins.

He had to smell like his brother.

How sad.

Yet how often do we do the same thing. We so long to be affirmed…to be accepted…to be valued…that we will wear whatever mask is necessary to get it.

We will succeed in school for the accolades that it brings.

We will strive in sports for the thrill of victory…and the sense that we are significant…that the trophies mean something…that the applause will last forever.

My dad was a golfer. He loved the sport. My oldest brother was an all-state golfer, loved and admired by my father. I was a wanna-be golfer, wanting to be good to prove myself.

I played in junior golf tournaments in Florida. Before every tournament, I was in the bathroom with a bad bout of irritable bowel syndrome. I thought I was simply nervous for a golf tournament. Looking back, I realize that there was more than just a golf trophy on the line. I was playing for my dad's approval. I was trying to measure up to my brother. I wanted my father's blessing.

How many people, especially men, make good grades…play sports…build their muscles…build their resume…strive to make money…climb the corporate ladder…simply to feel valuable…to feel like they mean something…to earn the elusive approval of their father.

Becoming something they are not to gain a blessing that is only a charade.

Jacob achieves his goal but fails to satisfy his soul.

Scene Four: Esau's Despair (27:30-40)

Esau re-enters the scene as Jacob quickly exits. He is carrying a tray full of savory venison, freshly killed, carefully prepared, respectfully presented to his father.

"Let my father arise and eat of his son's game, that your soul may bless me" (27:31).

"Who are you?" Isaac confusedly asks.

Esau is taken back.

"I am your son, your firstborn, Esau" (27:32).

Isaac trembles violently.

"Who?! Where is the one who hunted game and brought it to me? I ate all of it before you came, and I have blessed him—and indeed he shall be blessed" (27:33).

Esau cries out with a desperate, despairing cry. The hunter is humbled. The bold one is broken. The great one is reduced to groveling.

"Bless me! Me! Me also, O my father!" (27:34).

Isaac has already given priority to Jacob. The blessing is confirmed. God had overridden Isaac's intent...just as the oracle had stated. The blessing of Abraham...passed down to Isaac...would now reside on Jacob, the younger brother.

Esau continues begging and pleading.

"Have you only one blessing, my father? Bless me! Me! Me also, O my father!" (27:36).

Isaac consoles his favored son with a consolation prize blessing.

*Your dwelling will be
Away from the earth's richness
Away from the dew of heaven above.
You will live by the sword
And you will serve your brother.
But when you grow restless,
You will throw his yoke
From off your neck.* (27:39-40)

In other words, you will not receive the promised blessing of God. What you get in life will be by your own efforts. And your younger brother will develop into the nation that God will bless...protect...and exalt. But your descendants will not go down easily and will often be a thorn in their side.

In reality, I am not even sure Esau understood the blessing. He was so short-sighted and focused on his own gratification that he probably thought the blessing was some kind of guarantee of a long life of personal comfort. That's all he wanted anyway. The blessing of God...the formation of a nation...the promise of a Messiah that would bless the world...were the furthest things from his mind.

Of course, Jacob doesn't understand it either.

But the blessing assures him that he will...someday.

God would achieve His sovereign purpose...over the stubborn intentions of Isaac...despite the shrewd manipulation of Rebekah...even through a deceptive heelcatcher like Jacob.

That is the prerogative of grace.

Scene Five: Jacob's Departure (27:41-28:9)

The final scene brings the narrative to a close.

Esau is nurturing a vengeful hatred toward Jacob, consoling himself by imagining his younger brother being strung up like one of his last kills.

Rebekah is conjuring up plans to get Jacob out of Dodge...just for a few days...and still calling the shots with her husband and her son.

And Isaac is coming to terms with the fact that Jacob is the true inheritor of the blessing of Abraham...*the older would indeed serve the younger*...despite Isaac's attempts otherwise.

Jacob is basically in the backdrop…only responding to what he is told to do.

From this point on, the family will never be together again. Though in many ways, they were never together in the first place.

Rebekah, despite her best efforts to manage everyone's life, will never see her beloved son again.

Isaac will only appear in the narrative again to die…and to be buried by his sons.

Esau will continue marrying, making babies, making money, and making out better than he ever anticipated…despite the lack of the blessing.

And Jacob will begin his journey from home.

Though he has his father's blessing, he still doesn't know who he is.

He still doesn't know who God is.

He is alone…lost…empty-handed…empty-hearted.

In the perfect place for God to appear.

CHAPTER SEVEN
A STAIRWAY FROM HEAVEN
Genesis 28

In Genesis 28, Jacob, the heelcatcher, the momma's boy, the target of Esau's wrath, begins his hastily planned journey from home.

It is not an easy journey.

Jacob's family lives in Beersheba, in the far south of the land of Palestine, close to the Sinai Peninsula. Haran, where Rebekah's family lives, is in modern-day Syria, due north about 450 miles from Beersheba.

At an average of 20-25 miles per day on foot, barring any setbacks, it is a good three-week journey.

When Rebekah tells her boy to flee to Haran and stay there for a "few days," she has obviously forgotten just how difficult of a journey it will be. You do not get the impression from the biblical narrative that Rebekah has been back to see her family. You do not even get the impression that the little family of Isaac, Rebekah, Esau, and Jacob have traveled much at all.

The passing of time has shrunk the journey in Rebekah's mind…and when she last took it, she was riding in an entourage of camels, treated like a princess.

Jacob is afforded no such luxuries.

In recounting his journey many years later, Jacob says that he began his trek with little more than his walking stick (cf. 32:10). And we can assume that momma also packed him some limited supplies of food, water, and provisions.

But this was not a trip that Jacob was accustomed to or prepared for. He was a tent dweller, not a trail blazer. He was a strategic planner, not a strapping pioneer.

Plus, put yourself in Jacob's sandals. He has no GPS. No rest stops. No road signs. No street lights. No fast food joints. No Cracker Barrels. No Holiday Inns. He was probably traveling on or near a well-worn ancient path, the King's Highway, but even this put him in jeopardy of bandits and hoodlums, not to mention wild animals.

Plotting out the mileage from where I live, you are talking about a trip from Baton Rouge, Louisiana to Dallas, Texas. On foot. Over rough terrain. Alone.

The Bible says that after the first day of travel, *he came to a certain place and stayed there all night, because the sun had set. And he took one of the stones of that place and put it at his head, and he lay down in that place to sleep* (28:11).

You are in pretty bad shape when the best pillow you can muster is a rock.

This "certain place" is about fifty miles from Beersheba. Jacob starts off on a fierce pace…eager to get to Haran…eager to get as far away from Esau as possible.

He is literally nowhere…with no one…having nothing…no light…and no peace.

He has reached rock bottom…with a literal rock for his softest comfort.

It is in this moment that God reaches down.

Then he dreamed, and behold, a ladder was set up on the earth, and its top reached to heaven; and behold, the angels of God were ascending and descending on it. And behold, the LORD stood above him and said,

"I am the LORD God of Abraham your father and the God of Isaac, the land on which you lie I will give to you and your descendants. Also your descendants shall be

as the dust of the earth. You shall spread abroad to the west and the east, to the north and the south; and in you and in your seed all the families of the earth shall be blessed.

Behold, I am with you and will protect you wherever you go, and will bring you back to this land. For I will not leave you until I have done what I have spoken to you" (28:12-15).

Wow.

Jacob went to sleep tired, exhausted, depressed, discouraged, fearful, terrified.

But instead of a nightmare, he has a mind-altering, life-changing, emotionally-encouraging encounter with God.

Jacob sees three incredible things. The "beholds" alert us to each one of them.

First, he sees a "ladder," or perhaps, more accurately, a stairwell. The Hebrew word, *sullam*, is only used here in the entire Old Testament. It is difficult to translate, but most scholars believe that it describes a stairway, similar to the steps that would ascend the outside of an ancient ziggurat or temple. Only in this case, the stairway starts on the ground and ascends all the way into the clouds…into the heavens…as far up as Jacob can see.

Second, he sees the angels of God ascending and descending on the stairway. Jacob is not alone. Myriads of angels are near him…around him…watching over him.

Third, he sees the LORD! Not over the stairwell, distant from him in the clouds (as many translations imply). But rather over *him*! Right next to him. Close. Near. Immanent.

The God of heaven visited him on earth.

As if this is not enough, God speaks.

Jacob, I know you.

I know who you are. I know your grandfather and your father. I was there at your birth. I designed you. I chose you. And I planned your future. Your descendants shall be numerous and your impact shall be great. Indeed, in your seed all the families of the earth shall be blessed.

Jacob, I am with you.

I have been with you from the first day you entered this world. I have been walking beside you each step of the way. You have never been out of my sight...away from my love. Even in your darkest days...even in your most deceptive decisions...even in your most fearful moments...I have been with you. I have never left you. I will never leave you.

Jacob, I am watching over you.

You do not have to fear. I will protect you. I will guide you every step of the way. I will bring you back safely to this land...your land...the land I have promised to give to you and to your children. You are not in an unknown place. You are right where I want you to be. You are home.

You are mine.

God meets Jacob where he is...and He speaks to his greatest fears...and his greatest needs. And most incredibly, instead of coming to him with anger or a well-deserved rebuke, God comes to Jacob with grace. Amazing grace!

"God came to Jacob at his lowest point in order that it may be seen clearly that all is of grace, unmerited, undeserved favor."[17]

Every other religion in the world is based on the concept of humanity trying to reach God. Only Christianity tells the story of God reaching down to

---

[17] Iain M. Dugaid, *Living in the Grip of Relentless Grace* (Phillipsburg, NJ: P&R Publishing, 2002), p. 53.

humanity…coming into our world… extending grace to each one of us even while we are running away from Him.

We are all heelcatchers.

We are all trying to control things…make life work…get our way in our own way. And we want God to conform to us as well. We try to manipulate Him through religion. Or we redefine Him to match what we want Him to be. Or we flat out deny Him so that we can do what we want without the nagging sense of guilt or shame or accountability.

We are master heelcatchers… wearing masks…manipulating God…deceiving others…deceiving ourselves.

Or as author Brennan Manning puts it…we are all imposters, fake versions of ourselves…living in fear…consumed with a need for acceptance and approval… demanding to be noticed…and yet unable to experience intimacy because we are not only lying to others but lying to ourselves.[18]

But amazingly…relentlessly…God still loves us.

He loves the real "us" that we are afraid for others to see.

I know you. I am with you. I am watching over you. You are mine.

How can God do this? How can God suspend His holy and righteous judgment? Extend mercy and grace to us? Forgive our sin? Dwell with us in our self-focused, self-deceived, self-gratifying, self-justifying selfishness?

Does God really enter our world…your world…my world?

In the first chapter of John's gospel, Jesus revisits Jacob's dream and reveals its grander meaning. In the first "truly, truly" statement of John's gospel, Jesus says:

---

[18] Brennan Manning, *All Is Grace* (Colorado Springs, CO: David C. Cook, 2011), pp. 56-57.

Truly, truly, I say to you, you shall see heaven open, and the angels of God ascending and descending upon the Son of Man (John 1:51).

Jesus is the stairway from heaven.

God truly…bodily…entered our world…dwelt among us.

The Holy, Holy, Holy among the heelcatchers.

And He died for our sins…in our place…bearing our deserved judgment upon Himself. And He rose again from the dead…defeating sin, death, and Satan…so that we could have new life.

This is the God of grace.

This is the God of Jacob.

He knows you. Do you know Him?

I did not grow up in a Christian home. It was a good home. A moral home. But not a home that knew Jesus.

We went to church on Christmas and Easter…and I hated every minute of it.

I was often under the hard wooden pews…coloring in my coloring books on the hard wooden floors.

"When is this going to be over?" I asked my mom during one particularly long service.

"Oh, in about five more minutes. Just be quiet," she replied.

Little did she know that I had my new Mickey Mouse watch…and I knew how to measure five minutes. I watched and watched as Mickey's right hand began to move. One minute…two minutes…three…four…five…

I stood up. My head barely peeking over the pew. But my voice echoing through that old, high ceiling, stained-glass cavern of sanctimoniousness.

"It's time to go home!" I shouted.

The place became deathly quiet as everyone turned to look at me. In that moment, I knew that the service was not over…but I was.

That was my picture of church. Long. Boring. Dead.

A few years later, my oldest brother, Scott, would enter the military. Long greasy hair in a ponytail. Marijuana-glazed eyes. Dim-witted smile. Forfeiting his golf game. Going nowhere. Wasting his life. My dad escorted him out of the house and into the recruiting office.

While in the military…drunk…alone…watching the movie, *The Omen*…God got his attention. Scared him enough to sober him. Opened his eyes and his heart to the good news of Jesus Christ through a Navigators missionary.

Scott came back home a different person. Short hair. Gleaming eyes. Joyful smile. Singing songs. Quoting the Bible. Talking about Jesus.

I saw the change. It was undeniable. And I was drawn by the newness of his life…the boldness of his faith…the joyfulness of his heart.

At the age of twelve, I trusted in Jesus Christ as my Savior. My oldest brother by my side as I prayed these words…*God, I know I am a sinner. I know I cannot save myself. Thank You for sending Your Son Jesus to die on the cross for my sins. Come into my life. Forgive me. Save me. In Jesus' name. Amen.*

Grace. Undeserved. Unearned. Unfathomable.

Given freely by God through Jesus Christ.

The Way…the Truth…the Life.[19]

The stairway from heaven.

---

[19] John 14:6, Jesus said to him, "I am the way, and the truth, and the life. No one comes to the Father except through Me."

Immanuel. God come near.[20]

At this point, Jacob is just being introduced to the God of his grandfather Abraham and his father Isaac. He certainly has heard of Him…but He has not been a significant part of his life. God is an ambiguous, distant, irrelevant force in Jacob's mind.

But waking up from his dream, Jacob proclaims: *How awesome is this place! This is none other than the house of God and this is the gate of heaven!"* (28:17)

Jacob names the place *Bethel,* the house of God, and he sets up his rock pillow as a memorial, arranging it in such a way that he will remember it if he passes that way again.

Then Jacob makes a vow. A classic heelcatcher vow. Self-focused. Conditional. Hedging his bets.

If God will come through for me…protecting me…giving me what I need…bringing me back safely…then He will be my God. And whatever He gives me…I will give a portion of it back to Him.

It is probably the kind of faith that most of us practice.

"God, if you come through for me, I will serve You."

It is faith with a contingency plan. A vow with a well-written pre-nuptial agreement.

I will trust You if….

Thankfully, God knows all about our heelcatching ways. He understands our weak faith.

O ye of little faith!

And still He says….

---

[20] Matthew 1:23, "Behold, the virgin shall conceive and bear a son, and they shall call his name Immanuel" (which means, God with us).

I know You.

I am with You.

I am watching over you.

You are mine.

STEVE FOSTER

CHAPTER EIGHT
THE HEELCATCHER MEETS HIS MATCH
Genesis 29:1-30

Leaving Bethel, the "house of God," Jacob has a pep in his step…though not much spiritual depth in his heart. He has had an encounter with God, but he is still a committed heelcatcher. He is still trying to manage life on his own, still trying to figure out who he is.

In Genesis 29, Jacob makes it to Haran. The 450-mile journey is complete.

Now it is time to find his uncle…and find a wife.

By this time, Esau has already married three times (26:34; 28:9). He is not only a "man's man" but a "woman's man" as well. Strong. Confident. Studly. Finding a woman is not a problem for Esau. Finding a good, godly one is another story.

Jacob, on the other hand, doesn't seem to have much luck with women. Perhaps he dated a few girls here and there…we simply do not know. But we do know that he is a momma's boy and Rebekah probably hovered so close to him that no woman ever passed inspection. Besides, right motive or not, Rebekah is intent on Jacob marrying within Abraham's family line. She is weary and wary of the Hittite women that hang around their community…over-eager, under-dressed, and thoroughly pagan.

So Jacob arrives in the area of Haran on a wife-hunting trip. He is smooth-skinned but far from smooth when it comes to women. But like a sheltered kid arriving in the big city, he is all too ready to jump into the game.

In Genesis 28, three "beholds" capture the eyes of Jacob in his dream.

Behold! A stairway. Behold! The angels of God. Behold! The LORD!

Ironically, in Genesis 29, three "beholds" capture the eyes of Jacob as he arrives in Haran.

Behold! A well. Behold! Three flocks of sheep. Behold! Rachel!

As Jacob enters the city limits of Haran, he first sees a *well in the field* (29:2). It is probably a cistern in the ground, surrounded by stones to mark its location, with a large stone sitting on top of it, like a softball resting on top of a jar.

Around the well are three flocks of sheep, some grazing on the beaten down grass in the area, others lying in the dirt chewing cud. A group of shepherds are huddled together, leaning on the rock and chewing the cud with each other.

"Did you see the Rams' game last night?"

"No, the old woman and I were in a fight last night. She thinks all I do is lay around all day doing nothing."

Jacob recognizes an accent similar to his own and wanders over to them.

"Hey guys, where are you from?"

"We are from Haran."

"Do you happen to know a guy named Laban, part of the Nahor family?"

"Sure do."

"How's he doing? Is he still alive?"

"Yep. Doing well. In fact, take a look over there, that's his girl coming up the road now."

Jacob peers through the dust dancing in the sunlight and sees a girl in the distance with flowing hair and a slim figure leading a flock of sheep toward him.

Jacob speaks to the shepherds while still staring at the girl. "Hey guys, why are you standing around? Why don't you go ahead and water the sheep and get them back out to the pasture where they can eat?"

The heelcatcher is at work clearing the playing field. No sense in having to compete with some other young beau trying to score on a potential mate.

The shepherds are annoyed. "Hey bud, we will water the sheep as soon as enough guys get here to move this here stone. That's when we will water the sheep."

By this time, Rachel is near enough for Jacob to get a good view of her. Everything he saw in the distance looks even better up close. Black hair. Tan skin. Gorgeous face. Beautiful smile. Shapely figure.

The heelcatcher is instantly smitten.

Conjuring up a strength he didn't even know he had, Jacob goes into "beast mode" and moves the stone single-handedly. The tent dweller becomes a rock mover. Clark Kent becomes Superman.

And he immediately flies into action, drawing water from the well, bucket after bucket, watering the sheep while watering at the mouth.

Barely able to contain his excitement, Jacob embraces Rachel and gives her a kiss on both cheeks, weeping with emotion.

Frozen in shock and admiration, Rachel wonders what just happened.

"I'm sorry, I'm sorry. Forgive me," Jacob says, still catching his breath. "My name is Jacob. I am the son of Rebekah, your dad's sister. I just traveled a long way to get here. And I can't believe I found this place…that I found your dad…that I found you!"

"Will you marry me?!"

Actually that last line did not come out of Jacob's mouth…though it certainly entered his mind. This is love at first sight…or at least intense infatuation and a massive surge of testosterone at first sight. Jacob has never seen a woman so beautiful in his life. And suddenly his 450-mile journey was worth every single, muscle-aching, sweat-drenched step.

It often takes a woman to turn a boy into a man.

When I first arrived at college, at the age of 18, I could barely tie my own shoes. When you are a momma's boy, there is not much that you have to do on your own. My mom cooked for me, made my bed, cleaned my room, washed my clothes, took care of all my needs. I was spoiled rotten in many ways…and so ill-prepared for life on my own.

Ironically, the college I went to was 450 miles from my home. It was a small Bible college that I had never heard of…no one in my family had ever heard of. But they offered me a full-tuition scholarship, all expenses paid, and I accepted.

So at the end of the summer of 1986, I loaded up the extra-large trunk and the vinyl-ripped backseats of my wine-colored Ford Fairmont…with boxes, books, clothes, food, small appliances, and a cutting edge Commodore 128 computer… and headed off to Birmingham, Alabama.

I had no idea where I was going or what I was doing.

But God knew that I needed to get away from home in order to grow up.

As a young, naïve, "preacher boy," I entered a small Bible college of 150 students…with a ratio of about 2:1 guys to girls. If I was going to find a wife at this school, I was going to have to make my move quickly and beat the other guys at the well.

It was during my junior year that my R.A. (Resident Assistant) gave me a bit of inside knowledge before the semester began.

"Hey, Steve, there is a girl coming from my church in Huntsville, Alabama. You may want to get to know her."

I took the hint and waited for her to arrive. When she pulled up in her white Grand Am, I "happened" to be there to help her unload her car, carrying the biggest and heaviest boxes. Before the last box was unpacked, I asked her out on a date.

She said, "Yes." Phase one: complete.

But then the next day, she came up to me and said, "No." Phase one crashes and burns.

She explained that she had met a guy during the summer and was still technically dating him. She didn't feel right going out with me...even if it was just a friendly "welcome to Bible college" dinner.

I was disappointed...but I bided my time...and my friend kept tabs on her relationship with this other guy.

Soon I was told that the relationship had ended and I asked her out again after a game of billiards in the student rec center.

She again said, "Yes." This time I didn't give her time to change her mind. We went out for dinner right then.

I would like to say that the rest is history...that the relationship was smooth sailing from there on out. But, like any relationship, we had our ups and downs. We were on again, off again, for the next two years, trying to decide if we were too different from each other to be together or too complementary to each other to be apart.

Thankfully we decided on the latter.

And after close to thirty years of marriage, I can say that she has not only made me into a man... but also made me a better man.

There is a reason that study after study shows that married men live longer, are physically and mentally healthier, are more likely to be happier, recover from illness quicker, take better care of themselves and make better life decisions than unmarried men. And despite the culture's exaltation of the sex-filled, carefree single life, married men have better, more satisfying, more frequent sex too.[21]

As the Bible says, *It is not good for man to be alone* (Genesis 2:18).

Now back to Jacob and Rachel…

Rachel runs home and tells her father, Laban, about Jacob.

And Laban runs out to meet his sister's son, Jacob.

Laban certainly remembers a similar occasion many, many moons ago, when his sister, Rebekah, left in an entourage of camels to meet and to marry Isaac. It was a fond memory…not because his sister was leaving…but because the man who came looking for a wife brought a treasure trove of gold, silver, and precious gifts…many of which Laban still had in his possession.

Laban was probably hoping for a repeat jackpot.

Instead he came out and met a smiling, exuberant, slightly annoying young man…all alone…no camels…no money…no stuff. As Laban embraces Jacob, he probably hugs him tightly to see if there might possibly be a bag of coins underneath his robe or a thick wallet in his back pocket. But much to his chagrin…there is nothing.

"Ah, my wonderful nephew! My flesh and my blood! We are so glad that you are here! Come, stay with us, so that we can catch up on all that is going on."

And thus, the heelcatcher meets his match.

Not Rachel.

---

[21] Andrew Hess and Glenn T. Stanton, "The Health Benefits of Marriage," *Focus on the Family Findings,* September 2012. Also Jennifer Steinhauer, "Studies Find Big Benefits in Marriage," *New York Times,* April 10, 1995.

But Laban.

The smooth-skinned deceiver from Beersheba is about to be schooled by the slick-haired con man from Haran.

Jacob learns four lifelong lessons rather quickly with Laban.

Lesson #1
Don't act desperate around a con man.

A month into his stay with Laban, Jacob makes it pretty clear that he is a lovesick, smitten young man. And his work ethic has hit a new high as he looks for more and more opportunities to flex his muscles for Rachel and impress her family with his gentlemanly service.

If you want to see a man act at his absolute best…and do things which are almost beyond comprehension…observe him as he is trying to win over the heart of a woman.

There are three things that are too amazing for me,
Four that are beyond my comprehension:
The way of an eagle in the sky,
The way of a snake on a rock,
The way of a ship on the high seas,
And the way of a man with a young woman (Proverbs 30:18-19).

Laban observes…and sees this as an incredible advantage.

"Tell me, what I should pay you for all this work that you are doing around the house and in the barn and out in the field and with Rachel's flocks?"

"Nothing, sir," Jacob replies. "Just give me your daughter Rachel's hand in marriage. She is worth everything to me and I will work for you for seven years with her as my only reward."

Rachel swoons. Laban smiles.

Lingering in the background, Leah, Rachel's older sister, seethes. "Rachel, Rachel, Rachel. All the boys are falling all over themselves to get to her. The cheerleader. The prom queen. The beach volleyball star. Nobody notices me... especially with her around!"

The Bible describes Rachel, the outgoing shepherdess, as *beautiful of form and appearance*. Turning to Leah, her older sister, the Bible says, *Leah's eyes were delicate* (29:17).

Not much to go on...but one thing is for certain, if a guy is describing a blind date to you and says, "Well, she has nice eyes," then you are not assuming the best from an overall physical standpoint.

The Hebrew word to describe Leah's eyes is *rak* which can be translated as "tender, soft, delicate, or weak." Thus, there are at least three possible ways to interpret Leah's eyes, personality, and physical appearance.

1. She has *tender eyes*...possibly her most distinctive or only attractive physical feature.
2. She has *soft eyes*...being of a quieter, meeker personality. She was the wall flower compared to her extroverted, extra-perky, extraordinary sister.
3. She has *weak eyes*...having a noticeable physical defect that perhaps makes her extra-clumsy and hides her beauty behind big, thick Coke-bottle-type glasses.

Whatever the case, Jacob is not interested.

But he is overly interested in Rachel.

Just as Esau came into the tent many years ago, starving with hunger, grunting out, "Red stuff! Red stuff! Red stuff!" Jacob now stands in Laban's living room, ravished with love, blurting out, "Rachel! Rachel! Rachel!"

And just as Jacob, the heelcatcher, took advantage of Esau's weakness…Laban, the con man, is now going to take advantage of Jacob's.

By offering to work for seven years, for free, for Rachel's hand in marriage, Jacob is offering Laban a bridal price that was probably four to five times higher than the going rate. This is not lost on Laban. It would be like a young man walking up to a used car salesman and saying, "I really need a car right now and I have $100,000 cash in my pocket. Is that enough for that cool-looking red car over there with the shiny wheels?"

Jacob has revealed too much of his hand too quickly.

Carefully guarding his words, Laban does not technically say "yes" to Jacob's offer. Instead he says with a side hug and a big ol' slap on Jacob's back, "Well, I would rather that she marries you than someone else. So, come on, stay with me and keep on doing what you're doing."

Jacob hears, "Yes," and starts busting his butt, working hard, cleaning the barn, cooking meals, moving rocks, shepherding sheep, shearing sheep, shoveling sheep dung, and acting like Wesley in *The Princess Bride* to whatever Laban or Rachel asks. "As you wish."

And the seven years pass like just a few days because of the intense desire he has for Rachel.

Exhausted, excited, and eager for the honeymoon, Jacob comes to Laban with one of the most honest but crass statements in Scripture. "I have fulfilled my work for you. Give me my wife so that I can have sex with her" (29:21).[22]

---

[22] "The explicitness of Jacob's statement is sufficiently abrupt to have triggered maneuvers of exegetical justification in the Midrash, but it is clearly meant to express his—understandable—sexual impatience, which is about to be given a quite unexpected surprise." (Alter, *Genesis,* p. 154)

Laban says, "Of course, of course…congratulations, my son! Let's throw a big ol' party to celebrate this special occasion!"

Lesson #2
Don't get drunk on your wedding night.

The wedding feast is a humdinger. The guest list is long. The music is loud. The food is abundant. And the wine is flowing.

Jacob enjoys every minute of it…and probably drinks way too many wine coolers, as Laban keeps passing them his way.

As the party starts to wind down, Jacob suddenly cannot locate Rachel. He finds Laban instead.

"Hey dad. I'm pretty tired. Thanks for the party. I am going to go the tent. Can you find my bride and send her my way?"

Jacob stumbles into the dark, heading to his tent.

While he is undressed and lying down, a veiled woman appears at the entrance of his tent. The moonlight shines in from the back, highlighting the form of her body but darkening her face. He knows it is Rachel. Who else would it be?

This is the moment he has been waiting for.

Passion takes over. Few words are spoken. The marriage is consummated.

Jacob…exhausted, satisfied, and inebriated…drifts off into sleep.

The next morning Jacob wakes up. Staring up at the hanging folds of the tent, he is rested and content. His arm is around his bride. Her soft head is nestled against his smooth chest.

"Good morning, beautiful."

"Good morning, Jacob."

The Scripture describes the shocking moment with two words.

"Behold! Leah!" (29:25)

Lesson #3
You reap what you sow.

Pushing Leah away in disappointment and disgust, Jacob shouts, "What are you doing here? You are not Rachel!"

"I know. I am Leah. Your wife."

"No, you are not. I married Rachel."

Jacob quickly tries to relive the evening. The feasting. The dancing. The drinking. The talking with Laban. The stumbling to his tent. The making love with his bride. When did the switch happen? He remembers the veiled form in the tent. He remembers the passion, the kissing, the climax. Was that Leah?!

"How could you do this to me?! I thought you were Rachel."

"My dad said to pretend to be Rachel so I went along with it. He said that's the way it should be. The older should always get the blessing before the younger."

Jacob's head hurts. The words sting. The alcohol is still wearing off.

He storms out of the tent and heads straight for Laban's house. Bursting through the door, Jacob confronts him face-to-face…anger pouring through his pores.

"What have you done to me?! Was it not for Rachel that I worked for you?! Why have you deceived me?!"

Calmly Laban replies, looking Jacob in the eyes.

"It is not our custom here to give the younger priority over the firstborn."

Jacob's face twitches.

The heelcatcher has been caught by a greater heelcatcher.

The deceiver has been deceived.

The one who made his father a fool just played the fool.

The one who donned goatskins just became the goat.

Laban continued with methodical…slightly sympathetic…calculation.

"Let Leah enjoy this honeymoon week with you. And then next week, I will give you Rachel too…as long as you agree to work for me for another seven years."

Humbled. Humiliated. Heelcaught.

Jacob agrees to the terms of the con man from Haran.

Lesson #4
When you live life on your own terms, you will eventually have to come to terms with your own foolish stupidity.

Whoever digs a pit will fall into it,
And he who rolls a stone will have it roll back on him (Proverbs 26:27).

Do not be deceived.
God is not mocked.
For whatever a man sows
That he will also reap (Galatians 6:7).

Jacob has been working overtime to make life work…striving, conniving, contriving up plans to get what he wants, depriving others if necessary. And right when he thinks he has it all figured out, he finds out he has been snookered all along. He falls into the same pit that he had dug for others. He reaps what he has sown.

Mark it well. Trying to make life work on your own will eventually make life not work at all. And when you step on others to get further up the ladder, you will eventually be stepped on by others coming up behind you even faster.

All of it is in pursuit of the wrong things. The ladder leads to nowhere.

Whatever your idol is…whatever you think you can't live without…whatever you are pursuing in this world…will at some point turn around and bite you. It will betray you. It will disappoint, dishearten, and dismantle you.

Why? Because, despite its deceptive lure, an idol will not satisfy the true longings of your soul. Just like the bait on the hook, the temporary pleasure you derive from it will at some point disappear and you will be left with the pain of the hook…and the realization that you are no longer in control of your life.

You can't drink saltwater to quench your thirst…and you can't look for temporal things to satisfy an eternal longing.

Jacob has just been hit with a big ol' dose of reality and it will lead to a big ol' beautiful mess.

CHAPTER NINE
A BIG OL' BEAUTIFUL MESS
Genesis 29:31-30:24

W*ho shot J.R.?*

It was the biggest question of the early 80's.

Back in the day, there were limited channels and just a few TV shows that held the attention of America. *Dallas* was one of the shows that rustled its way to the top of the primetime heap.

Part mini-series, part soap opera, part nighttime drama…*Dallas* told the story of the Ewing family, an oil family with lots of money, lots of intrigue, lots of deception, lots of family secrets, lots of love triangles, and lots of power struggles.

It was a big ol' Texas heaping helping of family dysfunction…served weekly to an ever-increasing American viewing audience.

And it was not only America that tuned in. During *Dallas'* thirteen-year run (1978-91), it became the most successful TV show globally, being translated into 67 languages in over 90 countries.

Everybody wanted to see J.R.'s nasty, underhanded dealings…his wife Sue Ellen's struggle with alcoholism…his brother Bobby's tense relationship with his conscienceless older brother…his parents Jock and Miss Ellie's good-natured, naïve acceptance of their family dynamics… and the many mistresses, business partners, family members, and enemies that intersected with the oil-rich Ewings and their white-fenced, cattle-laden, Texas-sized South Fork Ranch.

And when season three ended with a mysterious person shooting J.R. in the chest, practically all of America wanted to know…and waited expectantly…for eight long months…with numerous guesses and theories…and official Las Vegas odds[23]…to find out…

Who shot J.R.?

The fourth episode in season four revealed the answer to the long-awaited, attempted-murder mystery. It also set the record for the highest-rated show in TV history with 76% of all U.S. televisions turned on tuned in.[24]

My family was one of the many families that tuned in that night.

I know our next-door neighbors watched as well, especially since they had two pit bull dogs named J.R. and Sue Ellen.

There is something about good ol' family dysfunction that draws us in…sort of like the rubber-neckers that pass by a multi-car accident. We know something bad has happened and something inside of us wants to catch a glimpse.

Tell someone a nice story of a family being kind to one another and you'll get a courteous, smiling audience. Tell someone a lurid story of a family that looks nice on the outside but has hidden secrets, heated conflict, backstabbing deception, and recently discovered sexual sins and you'll most likely get a curious, wide-eyed audience.

Leave It to Beaver is enjoyable to watch. *Dallas* is downright hypnotizing.

Reading Genesis 29-30 is more like watching *Dallas* than *Leave It to Beaver*.

Jacob's family dynamics would give the Ewings a run for their money.

However, Jacob was no J.R. That role would have been best played by his uncle, Laban. Due to Laban's underhanded moves, Jacob has two wives who can't stand

---

[23] Dennis McLellan, "Sonny Reizner, 81: Bookmaker of Exotic Bets, Like 'Who Shot J.R.?'" *Los Angeles Times,* December 13, 2002.

[24] www.history.com/this-day-in-history/millions-tune-in-to-find-out-who-shot-j-r

each other, a fourteen-year no-pay work contract, and a whole host of headaches to deal with.

The fun has just begun.

Let's take a look at the three major characters in this made-for-TV drama.

Jacob—The Passive Husband

Jacob is a defeated man. What started off as a dream on *Fantasy Island* has turned into a *Nightmare on Elm Street*.

He was head over heels in love with Rachel and dreamed of a wonderful wedding, a hot honeymoon, and a *gracias, vamos, adios* return trip back to Beersheba with a drop-dead gorgeous, family-approved wife by his side.

Instead he ended up married to two rival sisters in a bitter, long-standing war with each other. There is a reason that the Bible prohibits a man from taking two sisters as his wives[25]…and Jacob is finding out what it is. Leah and Rachel are in a constant cat fight and Jacob is caught in the middle.

So Jacob shuts down.

He becomes a background character in his own family drama. He says nothing… he does nothing…except have sex and father children. Lots of children. Twelve in all…in the span of approximately eight years. And not once does it say Jacob rejoiced at the birth of any of his children…or even got involved in their naming.

He has checked out.

He works during the day…clocks in…clocks out. Comes home and reads the paper. Falls asleep in his recliner while the increasing brood of children screams all around him. Then he goes to bed and wakes up and starts the cycle again.

---

[25] Leviticus 18:18, *Do not take your wife's sister as a rival wife and have sexual relations with her while your wife is living* (NIV).

Jacob's only recorded words in the seven years after getting hoodwinked by Laban come in Genesis 30:2. After Rachel demands that Jacob make her pregnant or she will die, Jacob seethes in red-faced anger and yells at her.

"Am I God?! He is the One who has made you infertile!"

Jacob is miserable and depressed, going through the motions of life. And behind his depression...as in the case of many men...lingers a toxic mixture of hopelessness, purposelessness, and restlessness...boiling over at times in outbursts of verbally abusive anger.

The passive, couch potato, beer-drinking man is often a defeated man, feeling powerless in the face of his shame and regret.

That is the picture of Jacob.

Starring next to Jacob is his first legal spouse...the one he didn't ask for and still doesn't want...

Leah—The Unloved Wife

Leah is the tragic figure in this drama, deeply in love with a husband who is detached, distant, and dismissive toward her. Picked up and transported into a different family context, Leah would probably be the most tender-hearted, caring, dedicated, loving wife and mother around. But, unfortunately, that is not her situation.

She is a sensitive woman in a senseless marriage to an insensitive husband.

Proverbs 30:21-23 describes four things that literally shake the earth and are almost unbearable to deal with...

- A servant who gets the power of a king (and thus abuses his power).
- A fool who has all his needs met (and thus continues to act like a fool).
- A servant girl who displaces a wife (and thus gains the husband's affection simply by being younger and sexier).

- And a married woman who is unloved (and thus frustrated in the one area that she longs to give her love).

A woman is designed to love. It is in the core of her nature. And she longs to be cherished…to be treasured…to be loved.

A man asks in the depths of his heart, "Am I strong? Am I competent?"

A woman asks in the depths of her heart, "Am I beautiful? Am I cherished?"

This is Leah. She is a woman longing to love and to be loved…but instead she has a deceased momma, a deceptive daddy, a prima donna sister, and a despising husband.

Just as Jacob longed to be affirmed and blessed by his father (and only tasted it when he pretended to be Esau), Leah longed to be held and cherished by her husband (and only tasted it when she pretended to be Rachel).

Leah unveils the brokenness of her heart in the naming of her children.

Reuben. Look at me, Jacob, I bore you a son.[26]

Simeon. God knows I am unloved and has heard my prayer.[27]

Levi. My husband will be attached to me now that I have given him three sons.[28]

But, unfortunately, Jacob becomes more and more detached from Leah with each child.

---

[26] "'Reuben' is construed as *r'u ben*, 'see, a son'" (Alter, *Genesis*, p. 156).

[27] "Leah's second son was named Simeon (*sim'on*) because the Lord heard (*sama*) that she was hated. The word play catches the true significance of the name, for it is one of many names etymologically related to the verb *sama*, 'to hear'" (Ross, *Creation & Blessing*, p. 509).

[28] "The naming plays on *yilaveh*, 'will join,' and Levi. Once more, Leah voices the desperate hope that her bearing sons to Jacob will bring him to love her" (Alter, *Genesis*, p. 157).

Judah. Now I will praise the LORD.[29]

With the fourth son, Leah finally turns her attention away from Jacob and onto the Lord. For a time, she finds the peace, security, joy, and love that she so longs for in her relationship with the Lord.

But, unfortunately, it doesn't last.

The birth of Leah's fourth son apparently causes Jacob to shut Leah out of the bedroom. Rachel, the favored wife, is increasingly unhappy with each successive pregnancy that her older sister has. And Jacob is simply uninterested in upsetting Rachel, being with Leah, and dealing with the annoying wordplays behind his first four boys' names.

Imagine the scene as Jacob rests in his recliner…reading the paper…and Leah begins to vacuum around the living room…correcting the boys as they smack each other with plastic shepherd's staffs.

"Look-I-Bore-You-a-Son (Reuben) stop hitting *The-Lord-Has-Heard-that-I-Am-Unloved* (Simeon) and *He-Will-Be-Attached-to-Me* (Levi) or you'll make *Now-I-Will-Praise-the-Lord* (Judah) start crying again."

Jacob tries his best to tune it all out. But Leah catches his face twitch out of the corner of her eye. It is the most creative nagging technique in the history of marriage.

But, unfortunately, it doesn't work.

Later, when the sisters' servants get involved in this crazy baby-making competition, Leah aims her name-calling tactics against Rachel.

---

[29] "The naming plays on *'odeh,* "sing praise," and *Yehudah,* 'Judah.' The verb Leah invokes is one that frequently figures in thanksgiving psalms. With the birth of her fourth son, she no longer expresses hope of winning her husband's affection but instead simply gives thanks to God for granting her male offspring" (Alter, *Genesis,* p. 157).

Gad. I am so lucky to have another son.[30]

Asher. I am so happy to have another son.[31]

And then...after Jacob reopens the bedroom door to Leah...in exchange for a sale of fertility herbs to Rachel...a few more children enter the family.

Issachar. I have been rewarded with another son.[32]

Zebulun. Now my husband will exalt me because I have given him six sons.[33]

Dinah. I have been vindicated in this battle with my sister.[34]

Wow. And you think your family is messed up!

Remarkably the Bible does not hide the dysfunction of this patriarchal family. In fact, it puts the dysfunction on full display.

Why? Because every family is dysfunctional in some way. And seeing the extreme in Jacob's family just reminds us that God isn't shocked or surprised with any of the messes that we make in our lives or in our families.

Reflecting on Leah's plight, I think of my own mom.

---

[30] "Gad (*gad*), meaning 'fortune.' Leah's exclamation at the birth was appropriate for the source of the name: 'what fortune (*bagad*)'" (Ross, *Creation & Blessing*, p. 512).

[31] "Asher's name is derived from *'osher*, 'good fortune.' ...This noun *'osher* produces a common biblical verb, *'isher*, the basic meaning of which is to call out to a lucky person, *'ashrei*, 'happy is he'" (Alter, *Genesis*, p. 159).

[32] "The word for 'wages' (or, 'reward') is *sakhar*, which also means a fee paid for hiring something. ...Thus, Issachar's name is derived from both the circumstances of his conception and his mother's sense of receiving a reward in his birth" (Alter, *Genesis*, p. 161).

[33] "Leah said, 'God has endowed me [*zeba-dani*] with a good dowry [*zebed*]; now will my husband honor me [*yiz-beleni*], because I have born him six sons'" (Ross, *Creation & Blessing*, p. 513.)

[34] "This note of triumph is carried through in calling her daughter, 'Dinah,' 'judgment, vindication'" (Wenham, *Genesis 16-50*, p. 248.)

She was the youngest of eleven children, growing up on the fringes of the Great Depression. Poor. Neglected. Unloved. Abused by her alcoholic father.

She was starving for love.

Then she met my dad.

He was a responsible young man. An athlete. A hard worker. A lover.

My mom was pregnant at age 18. She and my dad married shortly thereafter.

The babies kept coming one after another. Dad worked harder to support the family. Mom worked harder to take care of the family. There was little time for love. The best affection…perhaps the only affection…my mom received was during times of intimacy.

If my Dad and Mom were newly married during the present age, I don't know if she would have stayed with him. He was a good man but rarely around. Work consumed his time. Golf consumed his free time.

I will never forget the night we were sitting around the dinner table and my Mom suddenly got up from the table. She started to cry as she ran toward the back bedroom. No one moved. No one said a word. My Dad kept chewing his food.

I had no idea what was going on…I still don't to this day…but I knew my Mom was upset. I got up from the table and went back to her bedroom. I sat on the bed next to her as she continued to sob.

"Are you all right, Mom?"

"Yes, I am fine. Just go back and finish your dinner."

I sat there for a while. Unsure what to do. Then I listened to her advice and returned to the table. Everyone was still eating. The clanging of forks on porcelain plates was the only noise breaking the hushed silence.

That scene paints a small picture of our family life back then.

Eating together. Around the same table. But miles apart emotionally.

There were probably very few quiet evenings around the dinner table in Jacob's household. But I imagine that there were many nights when Leah left the room crying…and no one said a word…no one made a move.

That is the plight of Leah.

Now on to the co-star in this malfunctioning marriage…

Rachel—The Unhappy Wife

Rachel is endowed with great beauty…charmed in life…favored by her husband…but still desperately unhappy.

Underneath the veneer of outward beauty resides a deep insecurity. She wonders if the affection and attention will still be there if her attractiveness fades away.

The first recorded words of Rachel in Scripture occur in Genesis 30:1.

Feeling the pain of infertility…and envying the fetal fruitfulness of her sister…Rachel screams at Jacob, "Give me children or else I die!"

Only three words in the Hebrew language.

She is as emotionally hungry for children as Esau was physically hungry for "Red stuff!" She fears losing her favored status with Jacob…she fears losing the spotlight to Leah…she fears being out of control and uncertain of the future.

Life has always been handed to her on a silver platter…reflecting back her flawless complexion. She has always been first…always been favored…always been able to get what she wants. Now she has feelings that she doesn't like and that she can't simply whisk away.

She feels like she is dying.

Unable to change her circumstances and unwilling to wait on the Lord, she turns to quick remedies. She offers her servant girl to Jacob so that she can have surrogate children through her. She is so envious of her older sister that she will sacrifice her intimacy with Jacob for some kind of fertile victory over her.

And when her servant girl gets pregnant, Rachel volleys back in the baby name-calling war with Leah.

Dan. God has judged my case in my favor and has given me a son.[35]

Naphtali. I am in a great wrestling match with my sister and I have won.[36]

But the "victories" over her sister are empty...and Rachel knows it. Her heart is aching for her own child. She has demanded a child from Jacob...borrowed two children from her servant girl...but now, in humility and brokenness, she asks for a child from the Lord.

Then God remembered Rachel, and God listened to her and opened her womb (30:22).

Joseph. God has taken away my shame and given me a son...and I believe He will add to me another one.[37]

Holding Joseph in her arms melts Rachel's heart. For the first time, she has a sense of peace. The battle with her sister fades into the background. A calm contentment pervades her soul. And the season of bitter baby-making madness finally comes to a close.

---

[35] "The verb *dan* suggests vindication of a legal plea" (Alter, *Genesis*, p. 159).

[36] "The name of the second son, Naphtali (*naptali*), emphasizes the conflict motif more than any other of the names (vv. 7-8). Rachel said, 'A mighty struggle [*naptule elohim*] have I waged [*niptalti*] with my sister.' According to this explanation, the name carries the meaning, 'my wrestling'" (Ross, *Creation & Blessing*, p. 511).

[37] "With this name there is also a double word play, the first being an expression of joy loosely connected to the name by sound ('*asap*), the second forming the motivation for the name Joseph (*yosep*): 'May the LORD add [*yosep*] to me another son'" (Ross, *Creation & Blessing*, p. 514).

Jacob's family is a big ol' ugly mess. Yet God is present *within* the mess…hearing half-hearted prayers…loving the unloved…humbling the haughty…healing the broken-hearted…and blessing those who seem to deserve it less and less.

In the midst of our own messes, that is good news.

God specializes in redemption, sovereignly taking the rejects and discards of the trash heap and somehow transforming them into a work of art.

Just look at the cross of Jesus Christ. The cruelest, most violent instrument of execution designed by the depravity of man became the greatest, most precious instrument of salvation provided by the mercy of God.

God takes messes and makes them beautiful.

That is called grace.

CHAPTER TEN
COMING OUT OF THE WILDERNESS
Genesis 30:25-31:55

I felt "called" into full-time ministry when I was seventeen years old.

I had no idea what that meant.

I grew up in an old-line, traditional, boring church. I sensed there was something sacred about "being in church," but I did not understand what was going on. The people there did not seem particularly happy...and I wasn't particularly happy to be there either.

It was like going to the dentist. Something you had to do...otherwise your teeth would rot out...but not something you really wanted to do.

But the radical change in my older brother's life caught my attention. Shortly thereafter, I bent my knees...bowed my will...and opened my heart to Jesus Christ.

My brother discipled me...encouraged me to memorize Scripture...gave me good books...and lived the Christian life in front of me, alongside me. I grew in my faith quickly.

I started attending a little Baptist church in our little city. Classic Southern Baptist. Gold-cushioned pews. Wood beamed ceiling. Oak stained pulpit in the center of the stage. A small wall behind the pulpit, guarding the three-tiers of the choir loft. A baptismal tank situated in the middle of the back wall. A long, thin wooden cross plastered to the white sheetrock above. An organ and a piano framing the stage. Above the piano, a badge-shaped wooden board with five little shelves. Black cardboard squares with white numbers slid onto the shelves announcing the hymn numbers for the Sunday service.

Sundays at this Southern Baptist church were very different from my earlier church days.

"Hey Brother Bob, how are you doing?"

"Oh, I am blessed of the Lord!"

Everybody was "Brother Bill" or "Sister Sue." My first Sunday I wondered if everyone was related to each other.

The white Baptist hymnal, with gold lettering, sat in front of me…along with a King James Bible and an orange visitor card. A little golf pencil was the only thing that looked familiar to me.

The singing was peppy. The preaching had energy. The invitation was long. Over the years, I learned all twenty verses…or however many there were…of "Just As I Am" sung several times over.

I got baptized at the age of twelve, became a member, joined the choir, was recruited for two or three committees (which were loosely defined and rarely met), and became a budding leader in the youth ministry.

I was "all in."

During "youth week" each summer, they often had one of the youth deliver a "sermon" on Sunday night. At age sixteen, I delivered my first sermon. Actually it was more like a lot of Scripture reading interspersed with a story or a joke. I ended with a poem.

A year later, I sensed God's call into full-time ministry.

No visions. No angel speaking to me in a dream. Just a realization that I didn't want to do anything else. Previously, I thought about being a fireman (I liked the big truck) or a lawyer (I heard they made a lot of money) or a meteorologist (I liked George Winterling, the meteorologist on local TV). But now, I had a compelling desire to be a pastor.

The little church affirmed my desire and even licensed me to preach before I graduated high school.

Four years of Bible college and a few summer stints as a youth pastor and I thought I was ready to take on the world. I was a confident preacher who thought I knew a lot about the Bible and had an idealistic view of the way church should be.

If First Baptist of Dallas with its thousands of members would have called me to be their pastor, I would have accepted in a heartbeat.

How naïve I was.

Twenty years later, I was called to be the pastor of a small Bible church in Baton Rouge…a church with around eighty people in attendance on Sunday mornings…and I quaked in my Dockers.

Twenty years of ministry had humbled me, broken me, stretched me, tested me, exposed me, and prepared me to be a true shepherd of souls.

God had taken me through the wilderness.

The "wilderness" represents the seasons in our lives that we didn't expect and didn't want but definitely needed.

In Genesis 30-31, Jacob comes out of the wilderness.

Jacob's "few days" in Haran[38] turned out to be twenty years. He came to Haran with the shirt on his back and a night-time promise from God to be with him. Two decades later, he is older…wiser…humbler. Two wives, twelve children, and a mean ol' codger for a father-in-law have changed him.

The wilderness never seems like a gift when we are in it but…looking back…if we are willing to see…we realize that it was grace in disguise.

---

[38] Genesis 27:44, *And stay with him a few days, until your brother's fury turns away* (NKJV).

In the craziness of having cat-fighting wives and crying babies, Jacob faded to the background of his own family drama. But after the birth of Joseph, Jacob wakes up, stands up, and speaks up to his father-in-law, Laban.

"I am ready to go back home."

Haran was not home. It was where he met his wives, started his family, and made his career but it was never "home."

He knew God had promised to bring him back home someday and now he was ready.

However, Laban is not real excited about the news. Jacob has been the unwitting source of free labor and lots of prosperity. Laban, the con man, knows a good thing when he has it. And since Jacob has been "had" on many occasions, Laban thinks he can figure out a way to finagle this situation to his advantage as well.

"Please, please, my son, stay…stay….," thinking of his next sentence carefully.

"I have learned so much over these last years from you and, through lots of prayer and time with God, I have to come to realize that God has really blessed me because of you."

A little flattery and some strategically-sprinkled, spiritual-sounding "God phrases" are usually useful for a con man.

"Just tell me the wages that you want and I will provide it."

This strategy has worked well for Laban in the past. He has squeezed fourteen years of free labor out of Jacob through his naïve son-in-law's novice bargaining skills so it seems wise to give Jacob the first move in this little chess match.

And by all accounts, Genesis 30-31 is a chess match. The heelcatcher and the con man are making their moves.

Jacob's first move. "I am ready to go home."

Laban's first move. "Oh, please, please, my son, stay. Name your wages. I will raise your pay or provide whatever salary, health benefits, 401k, or vacation package you need."

Jacob's second move. "I have worked for your benefit for a long time. Now I need to do something for my own family."

Laban's second move. "OK. What does that mean? What do you want me to give you?"

Jacob's third move. "Don't give me anything. But if you want me to keep working for you, then just let me have all the speckled or spotted sheep or goats for myself. You know, the oddball ones. The ones that are few in number and easy to spot. Then when it comes time to determine what is mine and what is yours, it will be obvious to see."

*Laban's third move…*pausing for a second, rubbing his chin, plotting out his strategy, seeing if this move in any way exposes his rook, bishop, or queen. "OK. Let it be just as you said." Never quite saying "yes"…never giving away too much…never taking his hand off his piece until he is totally sure that the move is not only safe but also to his ultimate advantage.

Secretly, the master con man sends a quick text to his boys telling them to rush out into the fields, remove all speckled and spotted sheep and goats from the flocks, put them on a bunch of pick-ups, and drop them off in a field fifty or sixty miles from their main pasture.

Laban smiles at his son-in-law, puts his arm around his shoulder, and says, "C'mon, my son, let's go get a hamburger in celebration of our new work contract. I'll treat." While they walk to the local burger joint, Laban chuckles inside at how easy it is to wipe the floor with his smooth-skinned son-in-law. "I sure hope my grandbabies don't grow up to be this gullible and stupid," he thinks.

What he doesn't realize is that the heelcatcher has just won his first chess match against the master con man...though there are a few more moves left to play out.

Jacob's fourth move. Jacob takes branches from several poplar and almond trees and peels off the bark to expose the white underneath. He then places these branches in the water troughs of the flocks so that they would see these "speckled" branches before they mated.

Jacob's plan doesn't make any sense for the modern reader. Two things make it interesting.

One, Laban's name means "white" and there is a little poetic justice in the fact that Jacob exposes the "white" of the branches to take advantage of his father-in-law, Whitey.

Two, Jacob's mating strategy is based on an ancient superstition that whatever a female sees (mentally or visually) right before she conceives somehow affects the physical appearance of her offspring. It was a superstition that apparently kept females from thinking about dogs or donkeys or ugly men while engaged in intercourse.

If that's all Jacob's strategy was based on, then he would have confirmed his father-in-law's suspicion that he was even more gullible and stupid than he looked.

But later on in Genesis, Jacob reveals that his fourth move was based on a dream that God had given him in which all the flocks being born were streaked, speckled, and spotted (31:9-13). This divine revelation provided the true basis for Jacob's request. The reason he added the superstitious white streaked almond branches into the watering troughs reflected his heelcatching ways.

A heelcatcher always has a back-up plan...even when God is the One giving His word.

Several years later, if you would have driven past Laban's fields, you would have looked out upon a speckled, spotted sea of sheep and goats. It was Laban's Oddball Farm...and Jacob, the oddball son-in-law, now owned all the property.

Laban's fourth move. Laban gets extremely angry.

Laban was sure that his third move had won the chess match. Now he realizes that his third move gave Jacob his first checkmate in one of their many, typically overmatched, matches.

The con man has been conned.

Whitey turns red.

Laban is not used to losing a chess match and Jacob knows that the next move is probably going to be Laban picking up the board and throwing it at Jacob.

So Jacob makes his strategic *fifth move*. He picks up his pieces and runs!

While Laban is off at a sheep-shearing party across town, Jacob gathers his wives, his kids, his servants, and all his possessions, loads up his camels and his donkeys, rounds up his swarm of speckled and spotted flocks, and leaves Oddball Farm, kicking up dust as he accelerates onto the highway.

When Laban finds out several days later, his *fifth move* is to put his own camels in fifth gear and chase down Jacob's blob-like entourage. He catches them about 300 miles down the road.

But here is where God intervenes, giving the omen-heeding Laban a night-sweating dream that warns him that any harm to Jacob will result in his own demise.

After some tense conversation, a vain search for his stolen idol figurines, and the setting up of a memorial boundary marker, Laban reluctantly relents...accepts defeat...kisses his daughters and grandchildren goodbye...and returns home.

The con man finally checkmated.

Before the checkmate, Jacob gives a speech. It is actually written in poetic form in Hebrew. It is more like a song than a speech. But it wouldn't be a song playing on the inspirational or the soft rock stations. This one was an angry heavy metal song, if anything.

Jacob unleashes twenty years of frustration on Laban. (Maybe that makes it more like a country song, "I Picked a Fine Time to Leave You, Laban!"…with apologies to Kenny Rogers.)

What's my crime?
What have I done wrong to make you chase after me
As though I were a criminal?
You have rummaged through everything I own.
Now show me what you found that belongs to you!
Set it out here in front of us, before our relatives, for all to see.
Let them judge between us!
For twenty years I have been with you, caring for your flocks.
In all that time your sheep and goats never miscarried.
In all those years I never used a single ram of yours for food.
If any were attacked and killed by wild animals,
I never showed you the carcass and asked you to reduce the count of your flock.
No, I took the loss myself!
You made me pay for every stolen animal,
Whether it was taken in broad daylight or in the dark of night.
I worked for you through the scorching heat of the day
And through cold and sleepless nights.
Yes, for twenty years I slaved in your house!
I worked for fourteen years earning your two daughters,
And then six more years for your flock.
And you changed my wages ten times!
In fact, if the God of my father had not been on my side—
The God of Abraham and the fearsome God of Isaac—

You would have sent me away empty-handed.
But God has seen your abuse and my hard work.
That is why he appeared to you last night and rebuked you! (Genesis 31:36-42)

In examining the lyrics, we learn a lot about Jacob's experience in the wilderness…and about our own experiences in the wilderness as well.

The wilderness is a place of **physical discomfort**. Jacob recounts day after day of pain and exhaustion and night after night of restlessness and insomnia.

The wilderness is a place of **financial uncertainty**. Jacob basically toiled for nothing for fourteen years and then confronted constantly changing compensation for six years thereafter.

The wilderness is a place of **legal injustice**. Whenever there was any loss on the ledger, Jacob took the hit, even though he wasn't responsible. He was taken advantage of over and over by a boss who held all the power and a system which was devised against him.

The wilderness is a place of **emotional heartache**. Jacob was beaten down, discouraged, and depressed. He was afflicted like the Israelites in bondage and Job in his despair. He almost lost hope. If God would not have intervened in a dream, Jacob would have reached a point where he would have either permanently given up or perhaps even taken his own life.

This is the topography of the wilderness.

Those who have faced a dire diagnosis, an unexpected job loss, chronic pain, dysfunctional relationships, unfair treatment, social injustice, verbal or sexual abuse, personal failure, anxiety attacks, unrelenting depression, or nagging shame have all spent a season in the drought-stricken, frost-bitten wilderness.

Whenever we are in the wilderness, the two questions that naturally emit from our hearts are "why?" and "how long?" The two questions that seed the furrows of the Psalms.

If you were given the opportunity to write out the events of the next 10-20 years of your life, you almost invariably would write out the same things that I would. Good health. Abundant finances. Successful work. Joyful relationships. Respectful children. Wonderful vacations. Stress-free circumstances. Times of pleasure. Times of prosperity. Times of peace.

But practically none of us would include an extended time in the wilderness.

Cancer.

Crisis.

Cries of pain.

Conflict.

Catastrophe.

As Professor Ian Dugiad notes, "Invariably we want life to be easy and smooth. We pray and we plan as far as we can to make life go that way. But sometimes the best way for God to get our attention and move us on to new levels of obedience is through a breakdown of comfort."[39]

Jacob was stuck in Haran for twenty years because of his own poor choices, the deceptive and unfair schemes of Laban, *and* the sovereign purposes of God. Haran was God's training ground for Jacob. It was both the bed that Jacob made for himself and the seedbed that God planted him in.

The Jacob *after* Haran looked a lot different in the mirror than the Jacob *before* Haran. Flecks of gray hair. A receding hairline. Tired eyes. Creases on his face etched down into the very crevices of his soul.

The wilderness had changed him.

---

[39] Dugaid, *Living in the Grip of Relentless Grace,* p. 96.

Now he knows the value of hard work and perseverance. The tent dweller has become a field worker. The pampered momma's boy has become a seasoned veteran in the fires of life.

Now he knows the sting of selfish greed and deception. The heelcatcher has tasted his own medicine. He has been on the receiving end of manipulation, deception, and underhanded moves…thus he gains a firsthand understanding of the pain that he caused Isaac and Esau.

Now he knows the power and faithfulness of God. The one who kept God on a shelf…at arm's length…as a tool only to be used for his own heelcatching purposes…now has seen God's hand…experienced His grace…acknowledged His sovereignty.

The wilderness was God's school for Jacob.

And Laban was one of Jacob's toughest instructors.

Isn't it ironic that God often puts someone in our path who is just like us in order to expose our own hearts? The person who bothers you the most is often just like you in some particular way. What bothers you in them is often the reflection of you in them…if you are willing to look in the mirror.

The curriculum in the wilderness is designed to humble us, to test us, to teach us, and to prepare us for the place where God wants to take us.

And you shall remember that the LORD your God led you all the way these forty years in the wilderness, to humble you and test you, to know what was in your heart, whether you would keep His commandments or not. So He humbled you, allowed you to hunger, and fed you with manna which you did not know nor did your fathers know, that He might make you know that man shall not live by bread alone; but man lives by every word that proceeds from the mouth of the LORD. (Deuteronomy 8:2-3)

Jacob (Israel) went through the wilderness.

Israel (the nation) went through the wilderness.

Our Lord Jesus went through the wilderness.

In the midst of extreme hunger, exhaustion, and temptation, Jesus quoted Deuteronomy 8:3.

Man shall not live by bread alone, but by every word that proceeds from the mouth of God (Matthew 4:4).

It is the Word of God…the promises of God…the power of God…that sustain us in the wilderness. The Scripture is our textbook…and our life line.

Here are the final exam questions in the school of the wilderness.

Will I lean on my own wisdom or God's wisdom?

Trust in the LORD with all your heart
And lean not on your own understanding,
In all your ways acknowledge Him,
And He shall direct your paths. (Proverbs 3:5-6)

Will I live my own way or God's way?

Do not be wise in your own eyes.
Fear the LORD and depart from evil.
It will be health to your flesh,
And strength to your bones. (Proverbs 3:7-8)

Will I demand my own timetable or trust God's timetable?

Why do you say, O Jacob, and assert, O Israel,
"My way is hidden from the Lord,
And the justice due me escapes the notice of my God"?
Do you not know? Have you not heard?
The Everlasting God, the Lord, the Creator of the ends of the earth
Does not become weary or tired.

His understanding is inscrutable.
He gives strength to the weary,
And to him who lacks might He increases power.
Though youths grow weary and tired,
And vigorous young men stumble badly,
Yet those who wait for the Lord
Will gain new strength;
They will mount up with wings like eagles,
They will run and not get tired,
They will walk and not become weary. (Isaiah 40:27-31)

I remain confident of this:
I will see the goodness of the LORD
In the land of the living.
Wait for the LORD.
Be strong and take heart
And wait on the LORD. (Psalm 27:13-14)

We can trust the Lord of the wilderness.

He is strong.

And He is good.

And He will bring us safely home.

CHAPTER ELEVEN
WRESTLING WITH GOD
Genesis 32

enesis 32 is holy ground.

Of course, all of Scripture is holy ground…but Genesis 32 invites us to take off our shoes…pause in God's mystery and majesty… reflect on our own life…acknowledge our deep struggles, doubts, fears, and idols…and experience the blessing of God.

So take off your shoes.

Enter the story.

Consider the mystery.

In Genesis 32, Jacob literally…physically…wrestles God.

Let's back up and take this chapter one bite at a time.

Genesis 32 is one of the most significant chapters in the Old Testament. It sits in the very middle of Genesis 12-50…the second part of the Book of Genesis which sets the stage for the redemption of this sin-cursed world through God's unconditional covenant with Abraham.

Genesis 32 explains the origin and meaning of the name "Israel," the name of God's chosen people. It marks the climax of Jacob's life. Everything in Jacob's story leads up to this event…and this event changes Jacob's name, his identity, his focus, and his walk with God.

But understanding Genesis 32 is not without difficulty. It is one of the most mysterious and widely interpreted stories in the Old Testament. Some see it as a strange mythical legend...some as a psychological war only in Jacob's imagination...and others as an allegorical story about prayer. But when interpreted literally and theologically, it becomes a story for us all.

After twenty years in Haran, Jacob is finally on his way back home.

His traveling horde consists of his two wives...eleven sons...one daughter... numerous servants...and herds of sheep, goats, cattle, camels, and donkeys. They are like an amorphous amoeba meandering across a large petri dish.

If you thought your last family vacation was difficult, then you should consider Jacob's plight. The oldest of the children, Reuben, is in his early teens. Joseph, the youngest, is somewhere around five or six years old. Their journey is roughly 350 miles. Travel time for such a large group is perhaps two to three months. "How much further?"..."When are we going to stop?"...and "Are we there yet?"...had to echo in Jacob's ears too many times to count.

As Jacob entered the land of Palestine and began traveling near the Jordan River, God gave him a sign of His presence...a divine vision assuring him that his traveling camp was not alone. Jacob's eyes were opened and he saw that a second camp was all around him...the angels of God! Feeling a wonderful peace, Jacob named the place "Mahanaim," meaning "two camps."

Jacob needed this assurance because he was getting closer and closer to Esau's territory.

Without the luxury of Google maps and address searches on the internet, Jacob most likely encountered a fringe group of shepherds who either worked for or knew Esau and relayed the most up-to-date information that Jacob could get.

"Oh, yeah, we know your brother, Esau. He has become a very wealthy and powerful man. He lives near the Dead Sea. Everyone in that area is subject to him."

The moment of truth was near.

For twenty years, Jacob had carried a nagging thought in the back of his mind.

"Does Esau still hate my guts? And, more to the point, does he still want to spill my guts all over the ground?"

Jacob simply doesn't know. Has time healed all wounds? Or have the wounds festered and metastasized in Esau to a cancerous, murderous animosity?

Jacob sends a brief, humble, conciliatory message to Esau to find out.

To my older brother and lord, Esau.
I have been in Haran with our uncle for the last twenty years.
I have acquired flocks and herds while I was there.
I wanted to let you know that I am in your area.
I am hoping to find grace in your eyes, my lord.
From your younger brother and servant, Jacob (cf. 32:4-5).

The response back is not encouraging.

"We came to your brother Esau, and he is also coming to meet you…"

So far, so good.

"And four hundred men are with him."

Not so good.

This does not sound like a welcoming party coming with balloons and cupcakes. "Four hundred men are with him" has all the connotations of a small army coming with clubs and swords.

Jacob trembles in terror.

The Bible says that *Jacob was greatly afraid and distressed* (32:7).

The Hebrew word for "distressed" (*yatsar*) literally means "to bind, to be cramped, to be in narrow straits." It has the idea of being trapped, bound, stuck between a rock and a hard place. It is the claustrophobic fear of being confined in a tight space where you cannot turn to your left or to your right…like being squeezed into a dark, narrow MRI machine with no prospect of ever getting out.

Jacob cannot turn around…behind him is his uncle, Laban, still licking his wounds…and he cannot go forward…in front of him is his brother, Esau, presumably coming to inflict some wounds.

The blood drains from Jacob's face. His adrenaline rises. Anxiety permeates every cell in his body. The "flight or fight" response kicks in…but he has nowhere to flee and he is not a fighter. Therefore, as a default heelcatcher, he quickly improvises.

First, he divides his family and possessions into two camps. A few days earlier, he was praising God for "two camps"—his own little traveling "army" and the armies of God surrounding him. Now he is creating his own two camps…doing his best to minimize his losses. Jacob can't trust the invisible, ethereal angels to protect his whole lot so he figures that he will help them out by making two smaller groups. His thinking is simple, even if it is totally fear-based. "If Esau attacks and starts slaughtering one group, then the other group will have time to escape."

Next, he prays to the LORD. Jacob is too much of a heelcatcher to pray first. Better to try to manage your own mess before tossing up a desperate prayer to God as a secondary resort. This is the first self-motivated prayer of Jacob. Previously he has prayed in response to God's revelations to him…but now he is praying in response to his dire situation and extreme anxiety.

O God of my father Abraham and God of my father Isaac…

Jacob's own relationship to God is still in early development so he pleads to God based on his granddad's and dad's faith.

The LORD who said to me, "Return to your country and to your kindred, and I will deal well with you."

Jacob reminds God of his message to him in a dream before he started back to the Promised Land...hoping that the revelation was real and that God still remembered.

I am not worthy of the least of all the mercies and of all the truth which You have shown Your servant...

This is an understatement. Jacob has done pretty much nothing but rely on his own resources, make his own decisions, follow his own desires, and plot his own course. But God, in His great grace, remained faithful to Jacob and continued to walk by his side, guiding his steps and even overriding many of his missteps.

For I crossed over this Jordan with my staff and now I have become two companies...

Jacob reflects on where he was twenty years ago and he can only thank God for His goodness to him.

Deliver me, I pray, from the hand of my brother, from the hand of Esau...

Jacob begs for God's protection...and clearly identifies who his brother is in case God needs help in knowing and remembering his name.

For I fear him, lest he come and attack me and the mothers with their children...

This is a "fox hole" prayer...but it is a fervent one. Jacob loves his own life and doesn't want to lose it. He also loves his family and doesn't want to lose them. Jacob is hoping that God will act in defense of the women and the children if nothing else.

For You said, "I will surely treat you well and make your descendants as the sand of the sea which cannot be counted." (32:9-12)

Jacob again reminds God of His promise. If God is going to keep His word, then He needs to keep a wall of protection around Jacob and his children.

After saying "Amen," Jacob still has one more idea up his sleeve. He prepares a lavish, multi-herded gift for Esau, including 220 goats, 220 sheep, 30 milk camels (and their colts), 50 cows, and 30 donkeys. Over 550 animals…assembled in smaller gift packages so that Esau encounters them one…after another…after another.

This is a gift of enormous value. In today's language, Jacob is basically sending Esau gift after gift…of a new Ford truck…followed by a check for $25,000…followed by a Harley Davidson… followed by two Armani suits, a Rolex, and the latest iPhone. Each gift is presented with a gold-embossed message:

A GIFT TO MY LORD, ESAU, FROM YOUR LOVING SERVANT, JACOB, WHO CANNOT WAIT TO MEET YOU AGAIN.

Jacob's prayer to God is a good thing…but what he does before and after his prayer shows where his true confidence lies. Jacob sandwiches his prayer between two slices of his own heelcatching devices.

A heelcatcher is always trying to manage, manipulate, and control the people and the situations around them. God is often just one more tool to use and one more person to manipulate. A heelcatcher thinks, "I have my plans and I need to make them work. If I can somehow get God on board too, then that is all the better."

Jacob's embryonic prayer life reveals the true condition of his heart. His earlier lack of prayer showed his full reliance upon himself. Now his prayer to God in the midst of his own self-made schemes shows that his reliance is still on his own strength.

Previously Jacob had two hands managing his own life. Now he has one hand lifted partially toward the Lord while the other is frantically busy managing his own life.

Jacob is like many of us...casting his cares upon the Lord...and then reeling them back in so that he can fix them on his own.

However, in prayer, God wants us to learn to lift both hands...empty...clean... holy... dependent...toward Him.

Jacob still needs to learn this lesson in life.

That night, Jacob cannot sleep. He is restless, panicky, overwhelmed. He frets. He fidgets. He gets up and starts transporting all his wives, maidservants, children, and possessions across the streaming waters of the Jabbok, a small tributary of the Jordan River.

Finally, when they are all across, Jacob is alone. The blackness of the evening envelopes him...descends upon him...smothers him. His mind races with thoughts. His imagination runs wild. His breathing intensifies. His body tenses up. He suffers panic attacks...with wave after wave after wave of fear assailing him.

Then, suddenly, out of nowhere, he is hit...plowed over...knocked to the ground...

Before he can get his bearings, he realizes that he is in a wrestling match. A man is tightening his arms around Jacob's neck and squeezing...trying to pin him to ground...pushing his weight against Jacob's back.

Jacob musters his strength and fights back. Sweat pours from his face as he slips through the man's grip and searches for his own hold on the man's body. He drives his shoulder into the unknown assailant's midsection, flipping over and jerking the man's arm toward his back. The man twists and is seemingly face to face with Jacob. All Jacob can feel is the heat of the man's breath as he wonders who this man is and why he is attacking him. The mist of their breath intermingles for a moment until the man makes a rapid spin and applies a bear hold around Jacob's chest. Jacob pushes backward until they both begin rolling on the dewy grass.

When they stop, Jacob feels his head being jammed into the dirt by the man's forearm but he manages to grasp the man's beard and yank with all his might, plucking out a handful of long whiskers. In pain, the man releases his pressure ever so slightly. Jacob leverages the moment to pivot around the man and put him in a full nelson. Tightening his muscles and straining to drive the man into submission, Jacob feels a surge of strength like he has never felt before.

But then Jacob feels the slight touch of the man's finger on his hip. Instantly Jacob's hip is wrenched out of joint. Sharp pain shoots down his leg and up his back. Jacob screams in anguish but somehow maintains his hold around the man's shoulders…though now it is a grip of desperation rather than aggression. Jacob is holding on to keep the weight off his legs.

Finally, the man speaks, *"Let me go for the sun is beginning to rise"* (32:26).

This has been an all-night wrestling match. Jacob is drenched with sweat. His muscles ache. His right leg dangles limp from a dislocated hip. His arms are still dead-locked around the man's shoulder.

The next words out of Jacob's mouth shock even Jacob. *"I will not let you go unless you bless me!"* (32:26).

Jacob has longed for the blessing all of his life. More than anything, he has wanted to know who he was and what he was created for. He needed to know that his life had purpose…that he himself had value.

Wrestling all night had brought Jacob a strange feeling of release. Every muscle in him relaxed at once…except the muscles clinging to the Man.

And Jacob sensed that this was no ordinary man. He had felt the touch of his finger and knew there was a power inherent in this man beyond all human power.

As the darkness began to fade away, the light began to dawn in Jacob.

"What is your name?" the Man asked (32:27).

It was the question that has always plagued Jacob. Who are you? Who are you trying to be? Who are you pretending to be in order to feel accepted…loved…worthy?

But now there was no pretense. No mask. No goat skins.

"Jacob" (32:27).

The heelcatcher finally came clean. This is my name. This is who I am. Deceiver. Manipulator. This is the kind of life that I have tried to live. Struggling to make life work on my own. Now I am ready for a change. I am ready to relinquish control.

"Your name shall no longer be called Jacob but Israel for you have struggled with God and with men and have prevailed" (32:28).

The heelcatcher became the God-wrestler.

The manipulator became the "God-mastered man."[40]

The one who tried to claw his way through life now became the one who clung to God alone.

In weakness, Jacob finally found his strength.

In surrender, he finally found his purpose.

---

[40] G. Campbell Morgan, *The Westminster Pulpit,* vol. 7 (London: Pickerling & Inglis), p. 323.

In faith, he finally found his identity.

Now Jacob has one question on his mind. "Who are you? What is your name?"

The man smiles, *"Why are you asking for my name?"* (32:29).

Deep down, Jacob already knows. He has heard the voice before. But now instead of being in his dreams, God has entered into his very reality.

The Man blesses Jacob and then disappears.

And Jacob called the place, Peniel. *"For I have seen God face to face, and my life is preserved"* (32:30).

Jacob wrestled with God...with the God-Man...with the Angel (Messenger) of the LORD...with Jesus Christ.

In the womb Jacob grasped his brother's heel.
As a man he struggled with God.
He struggled with the Angel and prevailed.
He wept and begged for His grace.
He found him at Bethel
And talked with him there—
The Lord God Almighty,
The LORD is His name! (Hosea 12:3-5)

Though Jacob resisted, ignored, and ran from God all of his life, God pursued him...found him...loved him...blessed him...entered his world.

What kind of God does this?

The same One who pursued us...found us...loved us...blessed us...entered our world in the person of Jesus Christ.

God demonstrated His own love toward us in that while we were still sinners, Christ died for us (Romans 5:8).

This is the incomprehensible love of the God of Jacob.

This is the amazing grace of the God who loves heelcatchers.

It was during my own struggle with panic attacks that I came to this realization.

We are created to worship God, to be in relationship with Him. But because of sin, because of the selfish bent of our hearts inherited from Adam, we turn to our own way.

All we like sheep have gone astray;
We have turned, every one, to his own way. (Isaiah 53:6a)

Wandering on our own, apart from God, we seek satisfaction, meaning, significance in the things of this world, temporal things that can never satiate the hunger for eternal relationship.

As Augustine discovered over 1600 years ago: *Thou hast made us for Thyself, O Lord, and our heart is restless until it finds its rest in Thee.*[41]

For me, at an early age, public speaking became the primary avenue of trying to gain significance…trying to feel valuable…trying to obtain the blessing.

I gave a short memorized speech and sang a song at my kindergarten graduation.

Even at the age of five, I learned that speaking in front of people set me apart, gained accolades, made others smile, made me feel special.

It was a gift and a talent…but over time it would begin to take the shape of an idol.

John Calvin said that our hearts are "a perpetual factory of idols."[42] We are always seeking, manufacturing, and erecting false gods that give us a false sense of value, meaning, acceptance, and significance.

---

[41] www.goodreads.com/author/quotes/6819578.Augustine_of_Hippo
[42] www.goodreads.com/author/quotes/30510.John_Calvin

Growing up, I got involved in drama, had lead parts in church musicals, preached a revival, spoke at my high school graduation, entered into the ministry. My ability to speak well in front of people became intertwined with my very identity.

It was a good gift given from God. But I soon loved the gift more than the Giver.

In the midst of a stressful season in my life, I experienced light-headedness during one of my sermons. I felt like I could pass out. For the first time that I can remember, my ability to speak in front of others was jeopardized.

My hip was touched. The place of my strength.

Dig down to the roots of anxiety and you will usually find an idol buried deep in your heart. Something valuable…precious…beloved…a source of significance…meaning…strength. It is probably a good thing…even a gift. But it has so wrapped itself around your heart that you begin to think that you cannot live without it. It clings to you as much as you cling to it.

When this gift is threatened, anxiety rises to the surface.

Like a child holding on tightly to the side of a pool…while wave after wave is hitting them in the face…letting go seems like instant death when it is actually the way to freedom.

It is when our feet are knocked out from underneath us that we land on our knees.

It is when our hip is wrenched out of joint that we stop fighting God and start clinging to Him instead.

It is when our hands are empty that we finally experience the gift of grace.

The One Jacob thought was attacking him in the middle of the night was actually saving Him…saving him from himself.

The next day Jacob woke up with a limp. He was a new man. A man surrendered to the Savior.

A man with a new identity…a new attitude…a new hope…a new peace.

God had to cripple Jacob to bless him.

He had to cripple me to bless me.

He had to kill my pride…my self-reliance…my dependency on false idols…to give me life.

And He will do the same in you.

Because when we are weak, then we are strong.

Therefore, in order to keep me from becoming conceited, I was given a thorn in the flesh, a messenger of Satan, to torment me. Three times I pleaded with the Lord to take it away from me. But He said to me, "My grace is sufficient for you, for My power is made perfect in weakness." Therefore I will boast all the more gladly about my weaknesses, so that Christ's power may rest on me. That is why, for Christ's sake, I delight in weaknesses, in insults, in hardships, in persecutions, in difficulties. For when I am weak, then I am strong. (2 Corinthians 12:7b-10)

In November 2009, I was in the midst of a taekwondo graduation. I was testing sparring, basically an opportunity to "show off" your taekwondo moves in a simulated sparring match with an opponent.

My opponent was a sixteen-year old. I was forty-one years old…but feeling like sixteen again.

For my first move, I decided on a jump front kick…similar to the *Karate Kid* crane kick. Push off high from one leg and then kick with it while suspended in mid-air four to five feet above the mat. At least that was the way I pictured it in my mind.

But as I went to push off, it felt like someone crashed into the back of my leg. I quickly glanced behind me. To my surprise, no one was there. It was at that moment that my body pinpointed the searing pain in my Achilles' heel.

I collapsed to the ground...clutching to my leg...rocking side to side... grimacing in pain.

My sixteen-year old opponent stood there...shocked that he took me down without even throwing a kick.

Meanwhile I laid there on the mat...shocked that I had just ruptured my forty-one-year old Achilles' tendon in a taekwondo class.

The next six months would entail surgery, casts, walking boots, and lots of physical therapy. I had to learn how to walk again...running and jumping again would never quite be the same.

It was in February 2010 that I was called to be the senior pastor of Community Bible Church in Baton Rouge, Louisiana.

I preached my first sermon in a walking boot.

I began my ministry with a limp.

God's providential timing was impeccable.

His message to me was clear. "The only way that you can shepherd My sheep is by being totally dependent on Me. It is not your strength but Mine. And if you ever forget that, then just realize that you can be taken down in a heartbeat."

God cripples us to bless us.

We have this treasure in earthen vessels that the excellence of the power may be of God and not of us. (2 Corinthians 4:7)

We all live in *earthen vessels...jars of clay...*weak bodies.

We all walk through this life with a limp.

You can cleverly try to cover over your weakness with addictions, masks, and worldly success.

Or you can dependently clutch around the shoulders of your all-sufficient Savior...shoulders that bore your sin on the cross...shoulders that can carry your burdens today...so that you can experience the strength...the life...the blessing...you are looking for.

What choice will you make?

STEVE FOSTER

CHAPTER TWELVE
THE SWEETNESS OF RECONCILIATION
Genesis 33

When Liz and I were newly married, we were often bored. We did not have kids. We were away from our families. The internet was not around to offer immediate distraction and siphon away time. Shows on TV were limited. Our friendships were as well. So on many evenings we had free time on our hands.

We decided to play games against each other.

The first game of choice was Boggle.

Boggle is one of those games that is more skill than luck. There is no rolling of the dice or random chance during your turn. Instead you shake up a bunch of cubed letters until they fall into place on a 4x4 square. Then when the sand timer is turned upside down, you begin connecting the letters together, writing down as many words as you can see. Points are awarded to longer words and words that your opponent does not see. One game usually consists of three rounds.

After two rounds, I realized that I was overmatched. Liz was finding words up, down, diagonally, side to side, faster than I could get my bearings on the letters themselves. She was beating me soundly and I was getting more and more frustrated.

Men are competitive. Their competency can often be tied up in a game. If the game is pure luck that is one thing but, when the game measures some level of your intelligence and skill, it enters a whole different ballgame. And my wife was not only beating me, she was pummeling me...humiliating me.

At the start of the third round, I was determined to win…not the whole game but at least the round. I needed some kind of moral victory.

When the sand timer was turned over, I worked feverishly. Words were coming left and right. Finally, I was in the groove. My mind was churning with maximum efficiency. By the time the last piece of sand fell, I was staring at a sheet of paper with at least thirty words…good words…long words.

We read our words, marked off duplicates, and tabulated our score. I announced that I had thirteen points. Liz said she had fourteen. I couldn't believe it. How in the world did she beat me again? I certainly had read more words off my paper than she did…and I thought that I had eliminated more of her words than she did mine.

I asked immediately…and, in my recollection of the event, rather innocently…, "Can I see your scoresheet?"

Her reply was sharp. "Why? Do you not trust me?"

I should have taken the cue. No game is worth questioning your wife's trustworthiness…or subtly accusing her of cheating. But I was newly married… and not very bright in the husband department yet.

"I trust you. I just want to check your score."

She flung the cardboard score pad into my chest and stormed out of the room.

That was not a good sign. I knew immediately that our evening had changed. What started off as a night of playing games together was about to turn into a long evening of hurt feelings, awkward silence, and humble apologies.

But first, I checked her scoresheet.

She won.

Feeling humiliated, stupid, frustrated, and whipped all at once, I shuffled into the bedroom to apologize. The words were not easy to say. Even though I knew

I was wrong, it was hard to admit. Part of me felt justified to ask for a simple score check. The rest of me knew that I was simply acting like a jerk because my pride was being sliced up, diced up, and skewered on a humble stick.

"I am sorry, Liz. I was wrong. You were right. I am sorry that it seemed like I didn't trust you. Will you forgive me?"

I can't remember her response. I know at some point we worked it out and moved forward. I also know that we have never played another game of Boggle since that night.

One of the first lessons in Marriage 101 is forgiveness. Indeed, if you fail that lesson, then eventually every other lesson won't matter.

Ruth Bell Graham once said that "a happy marriage is the union of two good forgivers."[43] She was right. Living together in a lifelong marriage increases the chances of being offended and intensifies the need for repentance, forgiveness, and reconciliation.

Conflict is a given. Two people…different genders…different backgrounds…different ways of thinking…different personalities…different perspectives…different perceptions of the same event…equals a multitude of differences.

If the quality of one's relationships determines the quality of one's life (and all the social sciences affirm this is true[44]), then the ability to admit you are wrong, ask and give forgiveness, and seek reconciliation is the key to one's happiness and joy in life.

Heelcatchers inevitably have problems in relationships. They are always competing, always comparing, always trying to get ahead…whatever the cost. And the cost is great.

---

[43] www.goodreads.com/author/quotes/36835.Ruth_Bell_Graham
[44] Edward Diener, "The New Science of Happiness," *Time Magazine,* January 9, 2005.

Jacob has been wrestling with God, wrestling with himself, and wrestling with others all of his life. Now after a night of wrestling at the Jabbok, Jacob is humbled, broken, limping. He has a new name. *Israel.* God wrestler. But the name has another connotation. Not only one who wrestles God but also one who has been wrestled by God…mastered by Him.

Hebrew scholar Robert Alter comments on the name *Israel*:

> …Names with the *el* ending generally make God the subject, not the object, of the verb in the name. This particular verb, *sarah,* is a rare one, and there is some question about its meaning, though an educated guess about the original sense of the name would be: "God will rule," or perhaps, "God will prevail."[45]

In other words, the name "Israel" has an intended ambiguity. Jacob wrestles with God and with men and prevails. How? By actually being a person who is mastered by God and submitted to Him… recognizing that God always prevails.

When you fight God, you will always lose. He created you, sustains you, holds your very breath in His hand. He is omnipotent. You are mortal.

But when you realize your weakness and cling to Him in tenacious dependency, you actually prevail. You touch His heart. You experience His grace. You receive His blessing. The child that whines, complains, and resists a loving, disciplined parent does not win. But one that humbly submits to, sincerely thanks, and lovingly adores their parent prevails. Every parent knows that a loving, thankful, submissive, obedient, affectionate child can conquer their heart.

In God's economy, submission brings victory.

Just ask the Lamb of God.

---

[45] Robert Alter, *Genesis* (New York, NY: W.W. Norton & Company, 1996), p. 182.

So Jacob is a God-mastered man. He still has much to learn. His identity has instantly changed, but his heelcatching ways are still ingrained in much of his thinking and acting.

Genesis 32 began with Jacob trying to manipulate the situation and having panic attacks as he prepared to meet his brother, Esau.

Jacob thought the issue was Esau. In actuality, the real issue was God.

Until Jacob learned to submit to God, cling to Him, and seek His blessing alone, he could not relate properly to others. His heelcatching ways were his feeble attempts to grab from others what he could only receive from God.

Now that his relationship with God is settled...now that his stubborn will has been broken...now finally he is ready to meet his brother, Esau.

In Genesis 33, Jacob is still leery of his twin brother, Esau. He has lived with him for many years and knows that Esau is volatile, impulsive, and carnal by nature. Esau is also coming with four hundred men, which does not portend a gracious greeting.

So Jacob is leery but surrendered. The panic is gone regardless of what happens.

He gathers his family together and arranges them with Rachel and Joseph in the rear, perhaps because he loves them more, but also because Joseph is the youngest and the only child of Rachel at the time.

Then Jacob goes to the front to meet Esau first.

He bows to the ground seven times as he approaches his older brother. In Middle Eastern culture, a bow is not only a sign of respect but also one of contrition and apology. Jacob is acknowledging Esau's power, demonstrating his submission to him, and asking for forgiveness.

It is an expression of utter humility.

And if forgiveness and reconciliation are ever to happen, someone has to be willing to bow.

Esau surprises him with love. He runs to Jacob, embraces him, kisses him, rests his head on Jacob's shoulder, and weeps. Soon they are both weeping.

Reconciliation is sweet.

Twenty years of fear are gone. Twenty years of animosity are forgotten. Twenty years of separation are healed.

Esau meets Jacob's family...who each show the same humility as Jacob did. They are following his example...now in a good way.

Esau next asks about the lavish gift that was sent out in stages in an initial effort to pacify him. "What was that all about?" Esau asks Jacob...obviously oblivious to Jacob's ongoing fear of him and the ominous appearance of him showing up with four hundred men.

"These gifts were to find grace in your eyes, my lord." Jacob replies, still expressing humility, still treading carefully with his unpredictable brother.

"Oh, I have plenty, brother! Keep them!" Esau replies with a good slap on Jacob's back.

But Jacob insists, "No, please, if I have found grace in your sight, then receive them as a gift because seeing your face and being reconciled to you is like seeing the very face of God. Please, take them as a blessing because God has shown His great grace to me and I have everything I need."

The heel grabber has become a gift giver.

The blessing taker has become a blessing giver.

Seeing God face to face brought Jacob peace...being reconciled to his brother Esau brought release. The lingering tension was gone. The tightness in Jacob's shoulders...from carrying a twenty-year fear and burden...was finally loosened.

To give Esau a blessing, a *berakah*, not only acted as restitution for the stolen blessing but also as a fulfillment of Jacob's purpose. He was chosen by God not to grab, steal, and hoard blessings but to receive them graciously from God and give them generously to others.

One person gives freely, yet gains even more.
Another withholds unduly, but comes to poverty.
A generous person will prosper.
Whoever refreshes others will himself be refreshed. (Proverbs 10:24-25)

Feeling chummy, Esau invites Jacob to journey with him back to Mount Seir in the area of Edom. Esau surmises that Jacob's family needs his protection and doesn't have a particular destination in mind…so why not settle down in his territory. After all, what's better than a brother for a neighbor?

Jacob is caught in a quandary.

God has called Jacob to return home, to the Promised Land, to Bethel, the place where God first met him, and to the area of Beersheba, his old home, the place where he began his journey. Edom, to the east of the Jordan and south of the Dead Sea, is not where Jacob is called to go.

Jacob also knows that being with his brother, Esau, will not be best in the long run. Yes, they are reconciled but they are still vastly different…with different personalities…different goals…different kinds of families…different ways of living. Embracing each other is one thing…living together is another. Even the best of friends don't always make the best of roommates.

Jacob's response seems deceptive. He asks Esau to go on ahead and he will hope to catch up to him at some point at Mount Seir. The heelcatcher seems to be at it again.

But there is a sense in which Jacob's response is also a courteous deference, a way of saying "no" without directly saying "no." To refuse Esau's request flatly would "ruin the mood" and possibly lead to a long, hard to understand explanation. So

Jacob basically says, "Go on ahead, my lord. I have lots of children who are constantly needing bathroom breaks and I have a lot of young flocks that just naturally slow us down. I don't want to be a burden to you and your four hundred men who can travel so fast and unencumbered. You go on ahead. I will be much, much slower and hopefully I will see you at some point in Mount Seir."

Perhaps there was a better, more honest way for Jacob to answer, but he is not trying to be deceptive to harm Esau. Rather he is actually trying to be kind in not telling Esau, "Listen, brother, we are going different directions in life and you are not the kind of uncle that my children need to hang around too much."

Jacob is still growing, so it seems fair to give him a pass in this instance.

Esau next offers to leave some of his men as protectors for Jacob.

Jacob again refuses. "I greatly appreciate the offer, my lord, but I am just happy to find grace in your eyes. There is no need for you to burden yourself for my protection."

With that, Esau is on his way back to his home in Edom.

And Jacob continues his journey back into the Promised Land...with a prolonged pit stop in Succoth to rest his family and give his massive flocks a chance to recuperate.

Eventually Jacob crosses the Jordan into Canaan and pitches his tent outside of the city of Shechem. There he erects his first altar to the LORD.

El Elohe Israel.

The God of Israel is God.

Jacob has embraced his new name...and he has embraced the true God.

He is no longer just a heelcatcher trying to scratch his way through life.

He is now God's man…yielded to Him…worshipping Him…reconciled to his brother.

It is not incidental that Jacob's encounter with God and with Esau occur together. The great anxiety over his relationship with Esau leads to his encounter with God…and his encounter with God humbles him so that he is able to reconcile with his brother.

This pattern shows up in our own lives as well. Many of our heartaches, anxieties, and stresses come through our relationships with others. These conflicts often bring us to our knees, humbling us and leaving us clinging to God. From this position of brokenness and yieldedness we are finally able to admit wrongdoing, ask and give forgiveness, and seek reconciliation.

The toughest thing to conquer in conflicts is our own selfish will. Only when our will is conquered by God can we learn to submit to others.

In giving the Great Commandment (singular), Jesus gave two inseparable commands:

"You shall love the LORD your God with all your heart, with all your soul, and with all your mind." This is the first and great commandment. And the second is like it: "You shall love your neighbor as yourself." On these two commandments hang all the Law and the Prophets. (Matthew 22:37-40)

Love of God…love for one another…absolutely inseparable.

Relationship with God…relationship with one another…absolutely essential.

We were created for both. We are called to both. We encounter our purpose and joy in both.

If you want to evaluate your relationship with God, look at your relationships to others. It is easy to convince ourselves that we are "spiritual" and "godly." But our relationships with our spouse, our children, our siblings, our parents, our neighbors, and the people we encounter on a daily basis reveal the true condition of our hearts. If our will is unwilling to yield to others, then it still has not yielded to God.

If someone says, "I love God," and hates his brother, he is a liar;
for he who does not love his brother whom he has seen,
how can he love God whom he has not seen?
And this commandment we have from Him:
that he who loves God must love his brother also. (1 John 4:20-21)

If you are looking for peace, submit to God.

If you are looking for release, forgive your brother.

I have heard on a number of occasions from different Bible teachers that you do not have to forgive another person until they repent. The rationale is that God does not forgive us unless we repent so we do not have to forgive another person until they repent…until they come to us and ask for forgiveness.

I disagree. The Bible puts no stipulations on forgiveness.

Forgive us our debts, as we forgive our debtors. For if you forgive men their trespasses, your heavenly Father will also forgive you. But if you do not forgive men their trespasses, neither will your Father forgive your trespasses. (Matthew 6:12, 14-15)

Forgiveness is one-way. Reconciliation is two-way.

I can forgive from my heart regardless of the other person's attitude or response. But reconciliation only occurs when the other person repents.

This is actually the truer picture of God's forgiveness. God has already forgiven the trespasses of the world in His Son, Jesus Christ, the Lamb of God, who takes away the sin of the world (John 1:29).

Forgiveness is offered freely. The debt has been paid in full.

The issue is not forgiveness. The issue is reconciliation.

The unrepentant sinner is offered forgiveness but refuses the gift. Thus, he remains unreconciled to God. His debt is paid but...in his stubborn self-will...he chooses to bear the cost anyway.

Our urgent message to the world as ministers of reconciliation is not "Be forgiven!" but "Be reconciled to God!" (2 Corinthians 5:20).

Are you reconciled to God?

Are you reconciled to others?

It is tasting the sweetness of reconciliation with God that enables you to do the hard work of admitting your sin, asking and giving forgiveness, and seeking reconciliation with others.

It is bowing to God that enables you to bow before others.

Behold, how good and pleasant it is
For brothers to dwell together in unity!
Like the precious oil upon the head,
Running down the beard,
The beard of Aaron,
Running down on the edge of his garments.
Like the dew of Hermon,
Descending upon the mountains of Zion.
For there the LORD commanded the blessing—
Life forevermore! (Psalm 133)

STEVE FOSTER

CHAPTER THIRTEEN
THE STAIN OF ABUSE
Genesis 34

O ne of the TV shows that my wife and I used to enjoy watching was *Extreme Makeover: Home Edition*. Each episode began with a short video of a family sharing their story of heartache and special need. Usually their home situation added to the challenges of their lives.

After showing the video, Ty, the energetic, homebuilding, Good Samaritan, would assemble his team of merry homemaking men and women to go out and bless the family with an extreme home makeover.

The old home would be ceremoniously disassembled or destroyed and a new, better, more suitable home would be built in its place. The moment of "revelation" of the new home was always the climax of the episode. Tears. Shouts of joy. Hugs. Laughter. Oooos and ahhhhs. Everyone rejoiced in the gift of a new home.

When the episode ended, you went to bed feeling good about the kindness of human nature, knowing that a needy family was helped and, presumably, lived happily ever after.

That's how we like our stories to end.

And TV is good at giving us what we want.

But reality always tells the fuller story.

I read an article in the *Wall Street Journal* which followed up on some of these *Extreme Home Makeover* families. The results were not always good.

The article began like this:

Some families featured on "Extreme Makeover: Home Edition" find themselves in trouble once the cameras leave town. Some struggle to pay the upkeep on their expensive new homes while others tap the equity in their homes and end up with bigger mortgages that are hard to maintain. Some seek a quick-fix by trying to sell. But because Extreme Makeovers tend to be big, fancy residences plopped in working-class or rural communities, the houses can be a hard sell. "Like many homeowners in the nation, Extreme Makeover: Home Edition families aren't immune to the current state of the U.S. economy," said a spokeswoman for the show.[46]

The article went on to tell the tale of five families whose lives were almost made worse following their home makeover.

As someone commented regarding these failed extreme makeovers:

When you give an over-the-top house to someone that 1) usually has low or no income, 2) doesn't have much financial savvy (which often got them in the original predicament), and 3) can't afford to pay for the maintenance costs on a backyard carousel, elevator, $5000 oven, and many of the other things they put into these homes, it's a recipe for disaster.[47]

Not all stories end happily ever after.

Genesis 34 is sort of the reality check after Genesis 32-33. Jacob experiences a fresh new relationship with God in Genesis 32…receiving a new identity from the LORD Himself. And in Genesis 33, he is reconciled to his brother…resolving a twenty-year separation, with all its fears, assumptions, animosities, and anxieties.

---

[46] Dawn Motapka, "Extreme Stories," *The Wall Street Journal,* April 6, 2010.
[47] www.freemoneyfinance.com/2009/09/another-extreme-makeover-home-edition-home-being-sold.html. Comment posted on September 10, 2009.

Jacob is reconciled to God and to his brother. The reader is prepared for...*And Jacob lived happily ever after.*

Genesis 34 reminds us that this is not the case...and it is not the case in our lives either.

Jacob has had an extreme makeover. He has a new home...a new identity in which to live. But the same ol' patterns that got him into trouble in the first place still reappear.

Dr. Larry Crabb gives a good synopsis of this reality in our own lives:

> Our hearts are deceitful. A simple decision to surrender everything to Jesus may start a good process, but there are a host of hard, ugly things to deal with that we prefer to overlook as we keep on surrendering. We sometimes manage to persuade ourselves that God is as pleased as we are with our developing maturity, while in fact His Spirit is gently pushing open doors into the darker regions of our hearts that we pretend don't exist.[48]

There are dark, ugly things that come out in Genesis 34. Jacob's failures as a husband and father not only impact him but also his family.

Genesis 34 focuses on Jacob's daughter, Dinah. Jacob apparently had other daughters born in his family as time went on (cf. 37:35; 46:7, 15) but Dinah gets special mention because of the events which occur in this chapter. These events were impossible to forget in Jacob's life and in the lives of his family.

First, some context.

Jacob reconciles with Esau and then continues his slow, arduous journey toward Bethel and his father's house in Hebron, his ultimate destination. For some reason, when Jacob arrives at Succoth and later at Shechem, he delays his

---

[48] As quoted in Dan B. Allender, *The Wounded Heart* (Colorado Springs, CO: NavPress, 1990), p. 9.

journey, apparently by as many as ten years, enough time for him to build a house, buy some land, and for his children to grow up. (Joseph is around five to six years old when Jacob leaves Haran and is 17 when they finally settle in the Promised Land, Gen. 37:2.)

There is no explanation as to why Jacob halts his journey for this extended amount of time. Perhaps he was simply tired of traveling with such a large, chaotic, complaining horde. Or maybe he had heard from Esau that his mom, Rebekah, was dead and so his desire to hurry home waned. After all, facing his dad, Isaac, after all these years was going to be almost as difficult and awkward as facing Esau. Or maybe he just wanted to settle down for a while in a place that seemed safe.

Whatever the case, Jacob stops his progress toward Bethel. He gets comfortable, complacent, compromised. He builds an altar to God but fails to obey God. He experiences a new, passionate revival with the Lord but then reverts to his old, passive ways.

In the delay, Jacob's daughter, Dinah, develops into an attractive, socially-active teenager.

Dinah was one of Leah's children, one of the "second class" citizens in Jacob's family hierarchy. Rachel and her son Joseph were his clear favorites. The other boys, particularly the older ones, probably got the next slice of the pie. Then there was Dinah. Leah's daughter. Jacob didn't know how to show any affection to Leah...and probably didn't do much better with their daughter.

Now Dinah, the daughter of Leah, whom she had borne to Jacob, went out to see the daughters of the land (34:1).

Dinah is not even described as Jacob's daughter, only as the one whom Leah bore to him.

Growing up with a bunch of rambunctious boys, a depressed mom, and a distant father created a craving in Dinah's heart for relationship. So as the family lingers near Shechem, a town filled with pagan Canaanites, Dinah decides to hang out at the Shechem Mall with a group of giggly, iPhone-texting, selfie-taking, boy-flirting girls.

Jacob doesn't care...doesn't object...doesn't intervene...and probably doesn't even know Dinah has an iPhone.

But if Dinah isn't noticed by her dad, she is noticed by the Shechem boys, particularly the young prince of the city, appropriately enough named Shechem. Dinah's blossoming Semitic beauty makes her stand out...and makes her an innocent target...especially to a young man with power and a belief that whatever he wants he should get.

Shechem *saw her and took her and lay with her and raped her* (34:2).

This is the first rape recorded in Scripture and it makes your blood boil.

But then after sexually violating her, the Scripture says that Shechem's *soul clung to her...loved her...and spoke kindly to her* (34:3).

Such a diabolical dichotomy! Abuse then affection. Cruelty then kindness. Violence then tenderness. Holding her down in fierce passion then holding her in feigned compassion, comforting her from the very violent sexual act that he forced upon her.

The shame and confusion in a teenage girl's mind and heart had to be unbearable. From all implications in the text, she simply doesn't know what to do, so she stays at Shechem's house (34:26). Too ashamed to go home and face her family. Too scared and paralyzed to leave the room of her rapist.

> The victim of abuse is left thirsty and then is forced to participate in consuming something that both touches the legitimate thirst in her being while also destroying the very aspect of her being that has been relationally aroused. This catch-22 situation is awful. The betrayal is not merely the abuse, but also the upheaval of living on an internal roller

coaster that jolts the soul both toward death and life at the same moment.[49]

That is the bane of sexual abuse. It attaches shame and pain to a legitimate desire in one's soul. Yet Shechem has no remorse for what he has done. He simply wants to legitimize the rape in a lifelong arrangement where he can repeat the pleasure for himself.

Shechem speaks to his father, Hamor, the ruler of the city. *"Get me this young woman as a wife!"* (34:4).

Not one to rebuke or deny his lust-driven son, Hamor heads out to Jacob's farm to see if he can harvest some kind of deal.

Jacob hears the news of Dinah's rape and says nothing…apparently feels nothing as well. Maybe he is just shocked…or thinks she should have known better…or is just emotionally stunted and unable to enter into the darkening depths of the abuse.

But Dinah's brothers are livid.

The brothers have grown into young men…natural, emotional protectors of their little sister.

And the sons of Jacob came in from the field when they heard it, and the men were grieved and very angry because he had done a disgraceful thing in Israel by lying with Jacob's daughter, a thing which ought not to be done (34:7).

Jacob may not be much of a dad to his daughter…but her big brothers are going to stand up for their sister. They are *grieved and very angry,* cut to the heart with pain and boiling over with indignation. They clearly see the vileness of the violation and are ready for justice to be done.

---

[49] Allender, *The Wounded Heart,* p. 115.

Hamor, seeking to smooth over the situation, says that his son really loves Dinah, despite the evidence to the contrary, and genteelly asks for Jacob to give his daughter to Shechem in marriage...and to open the doors for peaceful, prosperous interaction and intermarriage between both of their peoples.

Shechem chimes in chivalrously with an offer to provide any price for Dinah's hand in matrimony.

Jacob remains silent. So the boys take over the negotiations...decisively... deceptively.

"Intermarriage sounds great to us," the brothers say in unison. "On one condition, and one condition only, all of your males, including you two, become circumcised like we are."

Hamor and Shechem have never encountered a request like this one...but being naïve to the whole circumcision process and eager to make a deal that requires no skin off their backs (just elsewhere)...they readily accept.

Convincing the rest of the males in the city to undergo such a sensitive surgery would seem to be a losing proposition. But Hamor and Shechem, already with considerable power and clout, couch the deal in the best possible light. "We will get to broaden our pool of potential mates and eventually absorb all of their property and prosperity into our own coffers."

So all the men of Shechem agree...and Hamor seemingly gets a circumcision doctor on the spot and quickly gets everyone to share their surgical misery together before they have time to reconsider.

Three days later, while all the men of Shechem are incapacitated in extreme pain in their extremity, Simeon and Levi unsheath their swords and slaughter them all, snatching Dinah from Shechem's house as they leave the city in turmoil and bloodshed. Then the rest of Jacob's sons descend on the city and plunder it.

It is an ugly scene.

Jacob finally speaks...and displays fiery emotion...but his speech is concerned only with his own safety and security.

You have troubled me by making me obnoxious among the inhabitants of the land...and since I am few in number, they will gather themselves together against me and kill me. I shall be destroyed, my household and I. (34:30)

Not the most inspiring of speeches...in the midst of the most tragic and most violent of circumstances.

The sons reply curtly. "Should he treat our sister like a harlot?"

In other words, "Forget you, Dad. This man raped *our sister*...violated her...defiled her. Should he get away with it? Shouldn't he face justice? Didn't he get exactly what he deserved...pain in his private parts and then a public execution?"

Most victims of sexual abuse probably see the poetic justice in what transpires...even as they lament the reality that sexual abuse and violence exist in our sin-cursed world.

Interestingly, God does not appear at all in Genesis 34. He doesn't stop the rape. He doesn't stop the violence. He is absent.

Sexual abuse victims often ask in anger, confusion, and sorrow, "Where was God in the midst of my abuse?"

In Genesis 34, God is weeping in the background...watching as a father fails once again to obey Him, lead his family, and protect his daughter...as a young girl hungers for love and flirts with fire...as an aggressive young man uses his power for his own gratification...and as a group of angry brothers avenge sin and injustice by creating even more sin and injustice.

God is not invited into the scene and so He gives them over to the consequences of their choices...and to the inevitable collateral damage that ensues.

Sin is ugly.

There is no way to whitewash it away.

And, as children of Adam and dwellers in this depraved, darkened world, we are all victims…and all perpetrators…at the same time.

It is the piercing pain of sin, addiction, abuse, tragedy, and violence that pierces our hardened hearts…drives us to our knees…and makes us thirst for a powerful, compassionate Redeemer… for a powerful, complete redemption.

I have come to see that more and more in my own life.

In the summer of 2018, the second wave of panic attacks hit me.

I was preaching on a Sunday morning…right after a relaxing, wonderful vacation…and I had another bout of lightheadedness.

It came out of nowhere. I thought I was as relaxed as I had ever been. Things in my life…and in my marriage…and in my ministry…were all good.

But the light-headed moment started the snowballing anxiety cycle in me once again.

"I thought I was past this," I reasoned to myself…in frustration and fear.

Stepping back, I should have seen it coming. I had not stopped in ministry for several years. A major flood in the Baton Rouge area in 2016 demanded a deluge of my time and energy. A year of numerous tragedies and deaths in our church in 2017 sapped my emotional energy. And the start of a multi-million dollar building project, along with staff transitions, counseling demands, and the expectations of a growing congregation, all piled up in 2018.

I neglected any kind of Sabbath in my life…after all, I was doing good things. But the lack of rest, the lack of sleep, the lack of healthy rhythms and boundaries, and the lack of true intimacy and dependency on my Savior finally caught up with me.

Something else caught up with me too.

The memories came flooding back unexpectedly. I was reading through an issue of *Christianity Today*. An article on pastors with sexual abuse in their pasts was one of the feature articles.[50] I started to cry...and to wonder, "How much has my own sexual abuse impacted me?"

Part of me thinks that I handled things well...moved on...closed that chapter in my life...made good choices to remain pure...found a godly wife...created a healthy marriage and family...overcame any ill effects from the abuse. But another part of me realized that the abuse had to affect me in some way...even if the signs and symptoms of it were not readily apparent.

I decided to dust off the memories of my past and open the chapter that I had sealed off those many years ago.

The shame, anger, guilt, questions, and confusion came rushing back.

I was in the sixth grade when I began attending a Baptist church in our small town. I went initially because I couldn't believe the trips that their youth group was taking. Ski trips. Mission trips. Trips to Six Flags. Our family rarely left Green Cove Springs. Our little town offered little in adventure. I was drawn in by the fun.

Soon I became a regular part of the church. I trusted Christ at the age of 12...was baptized...became a member...joined the youth group...started singing with the youth and the adult choirs. My mom started attending with me. It became like a new family to me.

The music/youth director was a charismatic, humorous, magnetic middle-aged man. He was married with two younger kids. Everything about him drew you to him. He had a way of making you feel special...valuable...loved. Being a pre-

---

[50] Joshua Pease, "When Pastors Are Sexual Abuse Survivors," *Christianity Today*, September 27, 2018.

teen with little relationship with my dad, his affirmation in my life meant the world to me. I had no idea where it would all lead.

What started off as conversations around the changes of adolescence, with him asking and answering questions that I was hungry to know, eventually turned into three years of sexual abuse.

Looking back, I can see how easily I was groomed for the abuse. He met a need I was longing for. He took advantage of my innocent curiosity. He used me for his own gratification…but then mixed in special trips, generous favors, and godly assurances to cover over his sinful violations.

He was "called" to another church when I was in tenth grade. The abuse ended. I was relieved…and confused…and ashamed. I determined to close that chapter and move on with my life. Pretend it never happened. Become more vigilant to make sure it never happened again.

It seemed to be over.

But right before I graduated high school, he was caught. At another church. Doing the same thing. As the web of deceptive abuse began to unravel, the strands reached back through several churches, through several years, through several young men. I was one of them.

The shame hit when I was questioned by two police detectives…in front of my mom…in the principal's office at the high school. I felt like I was on trial. I felt like I wanted to crawl under the table. I felt extreme embarrassment to have to discuss such matters in front of men who just wanted to get the facts…and my mom who was breaking down in tears. Later, giving a deposition in a sterile, brown-paneled court conference room with a bunch of lawyers and a court stenographer was no better.

It was a legal case. A big one in our small county. And I was just a pawn in the game to get a conviction and get the offender behind bars.

No one ever stopped to ask me how I felt…or if I was okay…or if I needed to talk. I probably wouldn't have wanted to talk, but it would have been nice to have been cared for…to be asked.

The church swept it under the rug and moved on.

I decided that must be the godly thing to do and did the same.

Only the stain…and the shame…remained.

I am just now allowing God to pull back the crusted-over bandages…expose the wounds…identify the infections…clean them out…apply His healing salve.

I do not know all the impacts that the sexual abuse had on me but I do see how it attached itself to a legitimate desire in my soul. My hunger to be valuable…to be wanted…to be affirmed…in a sense, to be blessed…was met by someone who then took advantage of those desires to gain access to me for his own selfish sexual gratification. Thus, a legitimate desire in my heart finds itself stained with pain, shame, and a hyper-vigilant fear of being taken advantage of and betrayed again. It can be hard to trust…hard to be vulnerable.

Shame is an insidious thing. It clings to you even when you try to shake it off. It speaks to you even when you try to silence it. It makes you feel like damaged property…like a dirty person. It drives you to hide…not telling you that it actually grows deeper roots in the dark…in the moist cave of secrecy.

I am choosing to bring it to the light…to the Light, Jesus Christ.

I shared with the elders at my present church. They gathered around me…wept with me…encouraged me…prayed with me…gave me time away from ministry to process things with a counselor.

Part of my therapy has been writing this book. Remembering the life of Jacob. Remembering the God of Jacob…the One who loves heelcatchers and heals the unloved…the unwanted, the forgotten, the broken, the abused, the confused.

People like Dinah.

People like you.

People like me.

It stormed last night. In the midst of the darkness of where I am staying, sleeping alone, the room I was in rattled and lit up with flashes of light. The rumblings of thunder. The strikes of lightning. The sound of driving rain. It was one of those storms that reminds you of your weakness, your vulnerability, your complete inability to control nature…control life…control the things that occur around you…as much as you would want to.

I prayed for the storm to end and for God to keep me safe. After all, as I am writing this book, I am alone…out in the middle of nowhere…surrounded by a forest of tall trees. A strong wind gust or a random bolt of lightning could easily change the course of events around me.

Thankfully, the storm passed.

I woke up this morning to a cool freshness in the air. As I walked through the woods, the peace was palpable. Nature had drunk in the storm. The air was cleansed. The birds were singing. Flowers and tree buds were starting to burst open. New life appeared…after the storm.

No one wants to go through a storm…especially one that shakes you to the core while you are vulnerably exposed to the elements.

But storms have a purpose.

They bring the rain.

They bring cleansing to the air, nourishment to the soil, new life to nature.

God is Lord over the storms…in nature and in our lives.

And, if we trust Him, we will find that after the storm there is a cleansing in our hearts, a nourishment to our souls, and the emergence of new growth and new life in our walk with Him.

CHAPTER FOURTEEN
THE STING OF DEATH
Genesis 35

When you reach the age of fifty, you find yourself looking back as much as you look forward. The simple reality is that you have more time behind you…more life lived…than time ahead of you…life still left to live.

It often creates a feeling of nostalgia.

Nostalgia is an interesting word. It comes from two Greek words: *nostos,* returning home, and *alga,* pain. So it literally means, "returning home pain."

Several centuries ago, nostalgia was actually considered a psychological disease that needed to be cured. When it affected soldiers far away from home, "compassionate" military leaders either tried to beat the nostalgia out of them or threatened to bury them alive.

Later, medical doctors would "advance" in their knowledge and use leeches to try to suck the nostalgia out of melancholy patients.

It makes me glad that I live in the present.

Nostalgia is a longing for home…more than just a childhood home or even a pleasant memory. Deep down it seems to be a longing for something more…a longing for Eden. A longing for peace, *shalom.* A longing for time to stand still…for aging not to affect the body…for the ravages of decay and death not to take everything that we love away.

When I return to my hometown today, it has changed.

I drive by the church I went to growing up which has changed names, pastors, and congregations over the years…the McDonalds which was the first fast food chain to enter our small city…and the courthouse buildings and city offices which are swallowing up more and more space on the main street. Meanwhile, on the other side of the road, empty parking lots and decaying buildings mark the place where a menagerie of car dealerships used to thrive but are now gone.

I pass by the old bank my mom used to work at…the building that was once an arcade where I played *Asteroids*, *Galaga*, and *Pac-Man* with friends…and the old Pete's Hamburger building which just couldn't compete with the new McDonalds several decades ago.

I drive by the large industrial building that was once Johns-Manville where my dad worked. At one time, its massive complex and manicured landscape dominated the city, providing jobs for hundreds of workers. Now, it is slowly rotting away. The building crumbling. Paint peeling. The parking lot broken up into chunks of asphalt. Weeds growing all around. A neglected monument of a bygone industrial era in the city.

I pass by my high school. It hasn't changed too much on the outside, but I know the teachers I had are gone. My classmates have all grown up…moved away… some have passed away. The time there can never be recaptured. It only remains in pictures, in memories, and old dusty yearbooks that no one wants to see.

When I come back to my house on County Road 16-A, I relive all the memories there. The house which seemed so big when I was seven years old looks so small today. The pool in the backyard has been filled in with dirt. The trees have grown up. The animals…the cows, the chickens, the rabbits, the dogs…are all gone. My parents have aged but are still going strong. But I know my time with them is limited.

That is always what hits me the most.

The passing of time and the reality of death.

God has put eternity in our hearts...but mortality in our bodies. Of all the creatures on the earth, we have a sense of time...the past, the present, the future...and a longing for eternal life...life without pain, sorrow, and death.

A longing for home.

In Genesis 35, Jacob finally comes home.

I wonder what thoughts entered his mind as he re-entered the Promised Land, returned to the place where God first met him, and stepped back into the home where he grew up...aching for his mom who had died while he was away...and reconnecting with his ever-aging dad who he never quite got to know.

Genesis 35 serves as the conclusion of the Jacob narrative. Jacob will appear several more times in Genesis 36-50 but the focus will shift to Jacob's sons and specifically to Joseph. Thus, this last chapter in Jacob's story serves as the bookend to his life and reminds us again of the faithfulness of God.

God disappeared in Genesis 34...or better, He was disregarded and disobeyed. Jacob knew his destination was Bethel but for some reason he lingered in Shechem. The consequences were dire for him and for his family. It is often our little choices...our "little sins"...that lead to the bigger problems in our lives.

We can blame God's absence, but it is often our abandonment of Him and reliance on self that gets us into trouble.

A man's own folly ruins his life
Yet his heart rages against the Lord. (Proverbs 19:3)

Despite the debacle of Genesis 34, God still speaks...still reaches out...still walks with Jacob. God takes the initiative to get Jacob back on track.

Then God said to Jacob,
"Arise, go up to Bethel and dwell there, and make an altar there to God,
who appeared to you when you fled from the face of Esau your brother" (35:1).

God reiterates the call and Jacob acts. The silent, passive Jacob of Genesis 34 takes a back seat as the active, God-centered Jacob finally takes the wheel.

Jacob tells his family to get rid of all the foreign gods and idols in their possession...apparently there were many more than the ones Rachel stole from her father...and to purify themselves and prepare themselves for the journey to Bethel.

Jacob declares his intent to his family:

Let us arise and go up to Bethel, and I will make an altar there to God, who answered me in the day of my distress and has been with me in the way which I have gone. (35:3)

Jacob takes the mantle of spiritual leadership in his family. Behind the inevitable groans and complaints of his children about picking up and moving again, there was relief and comfort in knowing that their father was once again being a leader in his decisions, being a priest in the home, being a man.

And they responded.

All the foreign idols, as well as the jewelry which was often fashioned into the images of gods and goddesses, were collected and buried under a tree near Shechem. Though the shame and stain of Shechem would remain for many years, the symbolic nature of removing false idols, burying them, and leaving them behind probably aided in the healing process.

And then they began the journey to Bethel, the house of God.

If Jacob was worried about the Canaanite tribes bothering them or attacking them, it was wasted worry. God had already put the "fear of God" in them and given them a mindset to stay clear of this traveling horde of wild kids, angry young adults, and oddball speckled animals.

When they made it to Bethel, Jacob built an altar...perhaps in the same place where God first appeared to him in a dream.

God had been faithful. Jacob left Beersheba in fear and uncertainty…with just a staff and a stitch of clothing to his name. Now he returned to the same place…close to thirty years later…with a new name, a new family, a new prosperity, and a new outlook on life.

Jacob named the altar, *El Bethel,* "the God of the house of God."

Jacob knew the place as the "house of God" when he was there thirty years ago…now he knew the God of the "house of God."

And then God appeared to Jacob again…not in a dream but apparently in human form.

God blessed Jacob, reminded him of his new name, and reiterated His promise to his grandfather Abraham, his father Isaac, and to himself.

I am God Almighty [El Shaddai].
Be fruitful and multiply.

Jacob had done well in this department.

A nation and a company of nations shall proceed from you,
And kings shall come from your body.

Certainly an encouragement to a man who often felt inadequate and weak in the face of conflict and difficulty.

The land which I gave Abraham and Isaac I give to you,
And to your descendants after you I give this land. (35:11-12)

The Abrahamic Covenant. The key covenant of redemption. God's promise of the land to the nation of Israel…and the promise of a multitude of descendants and a "Seed" (singular) who would bring blessing to all the families of the earth (cf. 12:1-3, 7; 22:16-18).

Then God went up from him in the place where He talked with him (35:13).

This verse gives the impression that God appeared to Jacob in human form and talked with him face-to-face. If that is the case, then Jacob was talking with the Man whom he wrestled with all night at the Jabbok. He was talking to Jesus, the very Seed who would one day be born into this world through the lineage of Jacob.

Jacob was speaking both to his Creator and to his own great-great-great-great…grandson. The very embodiment of the promise. The very incarnation of grace. The One who would die for him one day to save him from his sins. The Savior of heelcatchers…like Jacob, His forefather.

Let that sink in.

So at Bethel…the house of God…Jacob's faith is restored…the covenant renewed…the promise of a safe journey and prosperous family realized.

It seems that all is finally right and complete in Jacob's world.

But walking with God does not mean that we don't experience heartache, pain, and sorrow. The shepherd who loves us and leads us often takes us through the valley of the shadow of death. We do not have to fear…but we will still grieve.

This sin-cursed world is not our home.

Three significant people die in Jacob's life…in fairly quick succession.

First, Deborah, Rebekah's nurse, dies. At some point, she must have traveled to Haran to check on Jacob. She was probably sent by Jacob's mom, Rebekah, to be a help in raising his ever-growing brood of children and to make sure he brushed his teeth and took his vitamins each day. She remained with Jacob and his family and traveled with them. In many ways, Deborah was the last link to Jacob's beloved mom, Rebekah, who died while Jacob was in Haran. From all indications, Jacob never saw his mom again after he left on that fateful day after deceiving his father. Her plan for Jacob to be gone for a "few days" turned into almost thirty years. Mother and son, the inseparable pair, never saw each other, talked to each other, or embraced each other again.

Jacob wept uncontrollably as he buried Deborah beside an oak tree in Bethel. With her was buried all the memories that he had of his mom, Rebekah. Her hair. Her smile. Her voice. Her words of comfort. Her nighttime kisses. Her strong personality. Her unshakeable love.

The place Rebekah's nurse was buried was called *Allon Bachuth,* the oak of weeping.

Then, with the grief still fresh in his soul, his precious wife Rachel dies as she is giving birth to her second son.

What was supposed to be an occasion of unfettered celebration…the barren wife giving birth to a second son…the son she longed for and dreamed about…the twelfth son in the family… became an occasion of unimaginable lamentation.

As Rachel's life breath is leaving her, she names her son, *Benoni,* the "son of my sorrow." Jacob cannot bear the thought of being reminded of Rachel's death every time he calls his lastborn son. Instead he renames him, *Benjamin,* the "son of my right hand." Benjamin would never leave his side. He would forever carry the memory of his mom next to his dad.

Rachel is buried near Bethlehem…the place where another baby would be born who would bring the hope of resurrection and life to a death-plagued world.

And as if the heartache is not enough, Jacob finally does make it back home just in time to see his dad, Isaac, for the last time before he dies.

The timeline is unclear so we simply do not know if Jacob had several years, several months, or only a few days with his dad before he died. We do know that Isaac was practically blind and in poor health over thirty years earlier. He obviously had a strong constitution behind his weak eyes and sagging beltline.

There is no record of any conversations between father and son in these last days. Maybe Isaac was too old, too senile, or too incapacitated to even talk coherently. But I am sure that Jacob must have relived a mountain of memories as he sat next to his dad and watched him breath his last. Tears of failure and regret flowed down his cheeks…for the dad that he loved…the dad that he deceived…the dad that he never really knew.

Esau and Jacob buried their dad together.

The Hairy One and the Heelcatcher finally reunited with Laughter.

Only, on this occasion, all they can do is cry.

This is not how we like our stories to end. We much prefer the "happily ever after" ending. But those endings are reserved for fairy tales. Reality in this world ends in death.

Ernest Becker, in his classic *The Denial of Death*, says that we spend our whole lives trying to deny and distract ourselves from this reality.

> Man is literally split in two: he has an awareness of his own splendid uniqueness in that he sticks out of nature with a towering majesty, and yet he goes back into the ground a few feet in order to blindly and dumbly rot and disappear forever. It is a terrifying dilemma to be in and to have to live with. …Modern man is drinking and drugging himself out of awareness, or he spends his time shopping, which is the same thing.[51]

I was first confronted with death when I was around six or seven years old. My grandmother died and my parents took me with my siblings to her wake. For some reason, I was drawn to her open casket. I stared at her sunken face, her wrinkled, pale skin, her vacant state. She was a woman I barely knew but I

---

[51] Ernest Becker, *The Denial of Death* (New York, NY: The Free Press, 1973), pp. 26, 284.

remembered her alive. I remembered her talking, laughing, smoking. Now she was lying there…lifeless…silent…dead.

As I looked around, everyone else continued to talk, laugh, and even smoke. It was odd. I felt like shouting, "Hey everyone, grandma is dead!" I didn't understand much about death but I knew it was serious. I knew it was irreversible. I knew it was scary.

It was the fear of death that six years later would awaken my heart to my need for a Savior. I could pretend to be in control of life, but I knew I had no answer for death. Bowing my knees beside my bed with my brother, I prayed to receive Jesus Christ as my Savior…from sin…from judgment…from death.

But it was the death of my sister, Jill, that truly pierced my heart.

She was beautiful. Green eyes. Golden skin. Perfect complexion. Bright smile. And the beauty went through and through. She was tender-hearted. Quiet. Kind. Affectionate.

As the youngest of six children, I was often left in the care of my siblings. I don't remember many of these times with them…except the times with Jill. She invested time in me. She would organize full school lessons for me before I was old enough for school. She had me write my letters. Do simple math problems. Draw pictures. Connect dots. And each assignment would be graded and handed back to me with a smiley face.

That's why I will always remember the morning when I heard her screaming in the bathroom. I woke up first and saw her lying on the bathroom floor holding her head. I froze. My parents were soon there asking her what was the matter.

"My head hurts! My head hurts!"

Frantically, they tried to pick her up and walk her toward the door.

"C'mon. Walk, Jill. Stay with us."

My mom and dad cradled her, carried her, out the front door…and rushed her to the local hospital in the middle of the night.

I stood there in the hallway…not sure what to do…so I scurried back to my room and tried to go back to bed.

The next morning there were muffled voices everywhere. I followed them into the kitchen. All my brothers and sisters were awake and the conversations were centered on Jill. I didn't enter into any of them. Instead I shuffled into the living room and turned on the TV. I remember that it was a Saturday morning because cartoons were on.

I melded into the world of animation, vaguely aware that what was going on in reality was not something that I wanted to know.

Eventually, I was carted up to St. Vincent's Hospital in Jacksonville, FL. Our whole family was gathered in some kind of family conference room. We were all sitting there around a large brown table. The faces of my family bore the weight of the moment. A doctor came into the room and gave the prognosis. I don't remember what he said, but I picked up on the idea that my sister had a 50/50 chance of living.

When he left the room, I remember my mom saying with a quivering voice, "Well, if you have never prayed, now is the time to do so!"

I think a few prayers were said, but it was obvious that we were not a praying family. We went to church on occasion, but the God we gave credence to was not personal. He was not involved in our lives. He was a distant, ambiguous Being who you hoped could hear you and had some inclination to help.

The next few days and weeks I would be picked up from school and transported up to the hospital…mostly to sit in the waiting room and do schoolwork. I was too young to go behind "the doors" that guarded my sister's room. Eventually I do remember being able to go in to see her. She was bald. Markings were all over her head. Tubes were coming in and out of her mouth and in her arm. A constant beeping noise echoed in the sterile room. It was good to see her again. But I didn't know if she was there or not.

Miraculously she recovered. She had a massive aneurysm in her brain caused by a tumor that was growing in the lining of her skull. The little hospital in Green Cove let her lie on a gurney for three hours before they realized the severity of her condition. Apparently during the ambulance trip to Jacksonville they had to stop several times to make sure she was still breathing. When she finally did arrive at St. Vincent's, her life was in the balance. It could go either way...with the tilt being toward death or at least toward permanent brain damage.

But she not only survived...she also had no ongoing affects from the aneurysm.

God answered our muddled prayers.

But the possibility of the cancer returning lingered in the air. She went through several rounds of radiation to lessen this chance.

But thirteen years, a marriage, and two children later, the cancer did return. It manifested itself in a seizure that overtook her while she was breastfeeding her second son.

The battle began.

Surgeries. Radiation. More surgeries. More radiation. Alternative medicine. Prayers.

But each time the cancer was beaten back, it returned with a greater vengeance.

In the midst of the war, my sister, a woman growing stronger and stronger in her faith as her body became weaker and weaker in health, wrote these words.

It became her battle cry.

In the face of death
My heart trusts in Your grace.

In the face of life
My heart sees Your great power.
In the face of fear
My soul hides in Your strength.
In the face of doubt
My soul holds on to Your hope.
In the face of despair
My soul trusts in Your mercy.
In the face of pain
My life is kept in Your joy.
In the face of this battle
My soul lies in the Master's hand.

On Wednesday, March 6, 1996, my sister Jill stepped out of this world and entered a place where there are no more tumors…no more cancers…no more sorrow…no more death…only the glories and beauties of our Savior, Jesus Christ.

She made it Home.

Before departing this world, her desire was to see our Dad bend his knee to the Savior.

A month before she died, my Dad confessed his sin, confessed his need, and trusted in Jesus Christ as his Savior. He was baptized before my sister breathed her last breath.

Years later, with tears in his eyes…the first time I had ever seen my Dad cry…he gave his testimony to a group of men at our church.

He made this confession. "The only way God could get my attention was through the sickness and death of my daughter. It was when I realized that I was not in control of life that I gave control of my life to Jesus Christ."

He became a new man.

I can barely recognize in him the man he was when I was growing up.

My sister's death led him to life.

I still miss my sister.

I still see her at times in my mind's eye. Her green eyes. Her smile. Her laugh. Her love for me.

I have learned to hate cancer...to hate death. It is an enemy. It is an invader in our world...carried in by the cancer of sin.

But I have a Savior who has defeated sin...and defeated death. He died on the cross for our sins and rose again in triumph over death. There is no other Savior who has defeated death. If you find one, go follow him. As for me, I have cast my lot with the Risen One, the Seed of Jacob, the Savior of the world.

Jesus said these words at a funeral:

I am the resurrection and the life.
He who believes in Me, though he may die, he shall live.
And whoever lives and believes in Me shall never die.
Do you believe this? (John 11:25-26)

I do.

All of creation sings of His power,
Majestic mount to fanciful flower.
What will it take for you to follow Jesus?

His knowledge born in each man's heart,
Still we refuse to take our part.
What will it take for you to follow Jesus?

His Word proclaims it loud and clear,
But we don't allow our ears to hear.
What will it take for you to follow Jesus?

He loved you so much He went to the cross
Your life stands to gain for His took the loss.
What will it take for you to follow Jesus?

His invitation goes out to all men,
From the start of time so it has been.
What will it take for you to follow Jesus?

At some point in life it'll be too late
Your rejection of God will tell your fate.
What would it have taken for you to follow Jesus?

—Jill Foster, June 1992

CHAPTER FIFTEEN
THE LORD IS MY SHEPHERD
Genesis 49

Jacob is not much of a hero.

When we think of great men in the Bible...the heroes of the faith...the ones we read stories about to our children...we think of men like...

Abraham...the great man of faith who leaves Ur of the Chaldees to follow after God.

Moses...the strong Charlton-Heston-man who boldly tells the bald Yul-Brynner-Pharaoh, "Let my people go!" and then leads his people through the Red Sea and toward the Promised Land, receiving the Ten Commandments on Mount Sinai along the way.

Joshua...the leader of Israel's army who marches around Jericho until the walls fall down and then conquers the Promised Land.

David...the shepherd boy who slays Goliath, becomes king of Israel, and writes the songs in the Psalms that still minister to our souls today.

Or Daniel...the young captive in Babylon who remains faithful to God despite social pressure, who interprets dreams about the future, and who sleeps with lions who don't bite.

Then there is Jacob.

The smooth-skinned, tent dwelling, computer geek momma's boy who can never measure up to his all-state, all-hairy, all-man brother, Esau.

The deceptive heelcatcher who cooks yummy lentil soup to steal his brother's birthright and wears goatskins to deceive his father and steal his brother's blessing.

The passive husband and father who plays favorites, says little that isn't self-focused, and stays distant from his dysfunctional family as they grow in numbers, in conflicts, and in craziness.

As we read his story, we are more embarrassed than impressed with his life and his faith.

We don't teach our children to sing…

"Father Jacob had many sons…with two competing wives…and two misused maidservants…"[52]

Or "Laban, Laban, whoa baby, let Jacob's family go…"[53]

Or "Jacob's unfit parenting led to the battle at Shechem…"[54]

Or "When the Spirit of the Lord isn't upon my heart, I'm going to deceive like Jacob deceived…"[55]

Or "Dare to be a Jacob…dare to wrestle God…dare to say you're not Esau…dare to stop being such a fraud…"[56]

Yet God chooses to identify Himself as the "God of Jacob" on twenty-four separate occasions in the Old Testament…more than He calls Himself the God

---

[52] *Father Abraham*, "Father Abraham had many sons, many sons had Father Abraham…"
[53] *Pharaoh, Pharaoh*, "Pharaoh, Pharaoh, whoa baby, let my people go!"
[54] *Battle of Jericho*, "Joshua fit the battle of Jericho, Jericho, Jericho…"
[55] *The Spirit of David*, "When the Spirit of the Lord comes upon my heart. I will dance like David danced…"
[56] *Dare to Be a Daniel*, "Dare to be a Daniel, Dare to stand alone! Dare to have a purpose firm! Dare to make it known."

of Abraham or the God of David or the God of anyone else. And God chooses to call His chosen people "Israel," the new name given to Jacob.

We may wonder why.

I think it is because we are all heelcatchers to some extent...we are all trying to control our own lives...manipulate God and others according to our own agenda...scratch and claw to make life work the way we want it to.

And God's grace is shown in choosing us...loving us...changing us...despite our weaknesses...for His glory alone.

> Our God delights in writing straight with a crooked pencil. He delights in using clay pots in which to store his treasure. The reason for this is simple. His strength is most abundantly seen in our weakness, and his glory most apparent when he uses the most insignificant people to bring about his wonderful purposes (2 Cor. 4:7). In the lives of Isaac and Jacob, this principle is abundantly clear.[57]

Sing aloud to God our strength!
Make a joyful shout to the God of Jacob! (Psalm 81:1)

The life of Jacob does not end in Genesis 35. In fact, Jacob will live approximately forty more years after arriving back home in Hebron.

But the Genesis narrative will shift in focus in Genesis 36-50 to the life of Joseph, Jacob's favorite son, the firstborn of his favorite wife, Rachel.

The life of Joseph is one to admire and to emulate. He is everything that Jacob isn't in many ways...fully dedicated to the Lord, morally pure, faithful through difficult times, wise and strong in leadership, tender-hearted and forgiving in relationship. But these qualities come through the fires of refinement. Joseph starts off as the bratty, spoiled, richly-robed favorite son of his father.

---

[57] Dugaid, *Relentless Grace*, p. xiv.

Jacob...the one who suffered the pain of being neglected by his father who favored his older brother, Esau...ends up neglecting his own sons in favor of Joseph.

We often end up repeating the mistakes of our parents.

And, as we get older, we often end up suffering from the example we leave our children.

Jacob...the heelcatcher...the deceiver...is deceived by his own sons who, out of raging jealousy and hatred, sell their brother Joseph into Egyptian slavery for the bargain price of twenty shekels of silver (about $200). They then deceive their father into thinking that Joseph was torn apart by wild animals by dipping his multi-colored robe into goat blood.

The one who wore goat skins and served goat meat to deceive his father is now deceived by his own sons...with goat blood.

Like father, like sons.

But again, God in His sovereign grace overrides the sins of the father and the sins of the sons to accomplish His purposes.

In fact, Joseph would voice one of the most theologically rich statements in Scripture: *But as for you, you meant evil against me; but God meant it for good, in order to bring it about as it is this day, to save many people alive* (50:20; cf. 45:7).

God sent Joseph to Egypt...even through the selfish acts of his brothers...in order to refine his character, strengthen his faith, give him leadership in Egypt, and save his family, including his brothers, from famine.

It is an amazing story of God's redemption...and an amazing foreshadowing of a future Son of Jacob who would be betrayed and rejected by his own people but, through God's sovereign grace, would rise in power to save them.

But during the twenty-two years that Joseph is missing and supposedly dead, Jacob is not one to sing the praises of God's sovereignty, grace, and redemption.

Upon hearing the news of Joseph's alleged death, Jacob withdraws into a dark depression. He becomes inconsolable and declares, *I will go to my grave mourning for my son* (37:35). After losing Deborah, Rachel, Isaac, and now his favorite son, Joseph, in a short amount of time, he is convinced that God's hand is against him and that his life is nothing more than a tragedy.

"Everything is against me!" (42:36). The heelcatcher laments.

When it is finally revealed that Joseph is indeed alive...and not only alive but the second in command over the nation of Egypt...*Jacob's heart stopped* (45:26). The old man literally had a momentary heart attack in dismayed disbelief. But *the spirit of Jacob their father revived* when he realized that the news he hopelessly hungered to hear was actually true (45:27).

Jacob arrives in Egypt at the age of 130 (47:9). He lives another seventeen years in Egypt under Joseph's watchful care (47:28). Interestingly, Joseph was seventeen years old when his brothers sold him into slavery. One ancient Jewish commentator noted: "Just as Joseph was in the lap of Jacob seventeen years, Jacob was in the lap of Joseph seventeen years."[58]

Blessed are those whose help is the God of Jacob,
Whose hope is in the LORD their God! (Psalm 146:5)

When Jacob stands before Pharaoh as an old man, he describes his days as "few and difficult" (47:9). Time had flown by. And the journey was far from easy. Rejection. Jealousy. Doubt. Fear. Anxiety. Betrayal. Conflict. Sickness. Depression. Death. Jacob experienced all the ups and downs, successes and failures, triumphs and tragedies that a man could face on this earth.

---

[58] Kimhi. As quoted by Robert Alter, *Genesis*, p. 285.

But in recounting the great moments of faith in the biblical story, the book of Hebrews centers on one particular event in Jacob's life. An event that took place at the end of his life.

By faith, Jacob, when he was dying, blessed each of the sons of Joseph, and worshiped leaning on the top of his staff. (Hebrews 11:21)

Jacob's greatest moment of faith came as the final lines of his life were being composed.

In Genesis 48, Jacob is sick and in his last days. Joseph comes to him with his two sons, Manasseh and Ephraim. Hearing that his beloved son and two of his grandchildren are in the room, Jacob exerts all of his remaining strength and sits up in bed.

He recounts God's promise to him and his journey through life. Then he reaches out to bless Joseph's two sons, crossing his hands so as to place his right hand on the younger Ephraim's head and his left hand on the older Manasseh's head.

Joseph tries to correct him but Jacob insists that he knows what he is doing. Against expectation and convention...against the way man would normally do things...God puts his blessing on the younger.

God's ways are simply not our ways.

It is at this moment that Jacob speaks a poem...possibly sings a song...as he blesses Joseph's sons, worships God, and expresses the greatest moment of his faith:

God, before whom my fathers Abraham and Isaac walked,
The God who has shepherded me all my life long to this day,
The Angel who has redeemed me from all evil,
Bless the lads.
Let my name be named upon them,
And the name of my fathers Abraham and Isaac,

And let them grow into a multitude in the midst of the earth. (48:15-16)

Jacob, the recipient of God's blessing, gives the blessing to others. Instead of a heelcatcher... one who grasps at things for himself...Jacob becomes a blessing-giver...one who sees everything as a gift of God's grace and generously gives grace to others.

Jacob finally found his identity and purpose.

But more than that, Jacob finally found peace.

Looking back over his life, with all its crazy turns and emotional ups and downs, Jacob saw the bigger picture. He saw God's hand. He saw God's sovereignty. He saw God's beautiful design.

Jacob identifies God in two specific ways.

God is my Shepherd.

This is the first time in the Bible that God is described as a Shepherd...a theme that will become predominant and precious throughout the rest of Scripture.

Jacob was a shepherd. He understood how hard it was to shepherd. He even described the difficulties of shepherding in his emotional pent-up outburst against Laban.

There I was!
In the day the drought consumed me
And the frost by night,
And my sleep departed from my eyes. (31:40)

Shepherding is so stressful and strenuous because sheep are just so plain stubborn and stupid.

The most helpless animals in the world are sheep. If survival of the fittest is true, then there is no real explanation for the survival of sheep. They are dead meat unless there is a good shepherd nearby.

Sheep do not "just take care of themselves" as some might suppose. They require more than any other class of livestock, endless attention and meticulous care. It is no accident that God has chosen to call us sheep. The behavior of sheep and human beings is similar in many ways. ...Our mass mind (mob instincts), our fears and timidity, our stubbornness and stupidity, our perverse habits are all parallels of profound importance. Yet despite these adverse characteristics, Christ chooses us, buys us, calls us by name, makes us His own and delights in caring for us.[59]

Jacob finally got it. All the frustration he had in twenty plus years of watching weak, wandering, willful sheep was merely a small picture of what it was like for God to shepherd him.

Yet God loved him...cared for him...guided him...provided for him... shepherded him...as His own beloved oddball sheep.

All the great shepherding verses in the Bible owe their inspiration to Jacob's insight...and Jacob's life is perhaps the perennial example of God's great shepherding patience and skill.

The Lord is my shepherd,
I shall not want.
He makes me to lie down in green pastures.
He leads me beside still waters.
He restores my soul.
He leads me in paths of righteousness
For His name's sake.
Yea, though I walk through the valley of the shadow of death,
I will fear no evil
For You are with me.

---

[59] Phillip Keller, *A Shepherd Looks at Psalm 23* (Grand Rapids, MI: Zondervan, 1970), pp. 20-21.

Your rod and Your staff,
They comfort me.
You prepare a table before me in the presence of my enemies.
You anoint my head with oil.
My cup runs over.
Surely goodness and mercy shall follow me
All the days of my life
And I will dwell in the house of the LORD forever (Psalm 23).

Jacob also came to understand another truth about God.

God is my Redeemer.

Jacob describes God in three ways...the God of my fathers...the God who shepherded me...and the Angel who redeemed me.

The Angel of the LORD.

The Messenger of God.

The Word of God.

The Man who wrestled Jacob at the Jabbok.

This is the One who redeemed him.

The word "redeemed" is the Hebrew word, *ga'al.* This is another key theme used throughout Scripture but it is used first here...by Jacob.

Ga'al describes a redemption of all that is lost, a restoration of all that is messed up. And it is accomplished by a *go'el,* a kinsman-redeemer.

In the Hebrew culture, a person sold into slavery or land that was lost could only be redeemed by a kinsman-redeemer, someone related to you who had the power and the resources to reverse the situation and restore what was lost.

As a kinsman, they represented you, knew you, and loved you.

As a redeemer, they had the power, authority, and ability to save you.

Jacob looks back to that fateful night when he was overwhelmed with fear and anxiety. His world was crashing in around him. In his mind, everything he had was about to be lost. But through a midnight wrestling match with an unknown assailant and a crippling touch to his hip, Jacob finally learned the identity of his assailant and found his own identity as well.

The One he was wrestling against was God Himself.

What he was fighting all his life to achieve could only be received…in humble faith…from God.

Clinging in weakness to the God-Man, Jacob was redeemed.

God crippled him to bless him.

God humbled him to save him.

God wrestled him to redeem him.

And this God-Man Redeemer was Jesus Christ.

The coming Savior and Seed of Abraham, Isaac, and Jacob.

The Good Shepherd who would give His life for His sheep...for heelcatchers like Jacob.

The thief does not come except to steal, and to kill, and to destroy.
I have come that they may have life,
And that they may have it more abundantly.
I am the good shepherd.
The good shepherd gives His life for the sheep. (John 10:10-11)

Looking back over my own life, I can see God's hand. He has guided me…protected me…led me…and even made me lie down so that I can learn to rest in His care.

He is my Shepherd.

I am thankful that at the age of twelve, He reached down in His grace to save me by drawing me to His Son, Jesus Christ.

He is my Redeemer.

I do not know how much life is ahead of me. I do not know what events lie in my future.

But I do know that He can be trusted.

The God of Jacob…the God of heelcatchers…created us…knows us…loves us.

He has proven that once for all on the cross.

The God who can love Jacob can love anyone.

Even you.

Even me.

Be still and know that I am God.
I will be exalted among the nations.
I will be exalted in the earth!
The LORD of hosts is with us.
The God of Jacob is our refuge.
Selah. (Psalm 46:10-11)

EPILOGUE
GIFTS OF GRACE

If you want to see evidence of the power of the gospel of Jesus Christ, then all you have to do is look at my family.

A marijuana-smoking hippie goes into the military, gets drunk, and finds himself watching *The Omen* and being scared of the end times. He bends his knee to Jesus Christ as his Savior.

A young, vibrant seventeen-year old girl suffers a major brain aneurysm and does not get medical attention for approximately five hours. She not only survives but has no permanent brain damage. Changed by the event, she trusts in Jesus Christ as her Savior.

A hard-working, emotionally-absent husband and father watches the unshakeable faith of his daughter, that grown up seventeen-year old girl, in the face of recurrent brain cancer. Finally realizing that he is not in control of life or death, he bows his will…his heart…his knee to Jesus Christ.

My mom, an abuse survivor, found her strength, song, and salvation in Jesus Christ. She now enjoys a sixty-plus year marriage to my dad who is a new man…a loving husband and father who loves, cares, prays for and cries for his family.

My other two sisters trusted in Jesus Christ as their Savior.

My other brother trusted in Jesus Christ as his Savior.

I trusted in Jesus Christ as my Savior.

A family that knew absolutely nothing about the gospel of Jesus Christ forty years ago is totally changed and shaped by it today.

As the lastborn "surprise" child, who often felt like a spectator in the family, I actually had a front row seat watching the power of Christ move through our family.

I am forever grateful.

In 1998, I wrote a tribute to God for my family. This tribute seems like the appropriate way to bring this book to a close.

May God encourage your heart as you stop and reflect on His abundant gifts of grace in your own life. *Selah.*

---

5 A.M. No noise. No activity. Quiet, except for the ticking of the clock above the mantle. I'm up early. I couldn't sleep. The excitement of Christmas still gets me out of bed before the sun cracks the horizon.

I sit on the couch and stare at the lights dancing across the Christmas tree. Their colors reflect off the blackened windows like the memories in my mind.

A mountain of gifts surrounds the tree, a kaleidoscope of gold ribbons, Santa Claus smiles, green wreaths, reindeer, and snowmen.

I move closer. The smell of plastic and pine occupies my nose. Like a child, I search for the gifts addressed to me. Rearranging stacks and excavating through the mound, I pull out a heavy square box wrapped in plain paper...

FROM SCOTT.

A book. I know it. My library bulges with books from my brother, each with a handwritten message of optimism and admonishment. "Stay strong, brother, even when the road proves difficult, our God abides faithful."

A message from the prophet.

The former hippie, greasy ponytail, absent eyes, dumb-witted smile, a room full of heavy metal eight-track tapes and black lights highlighting psychedelic fluorescent forms on the wall. Marijuana his master. Transformed by the Holy Spirit to the prophet, his voice thundering out the Word of the Lord, his eyes penetrating to the heart, his olive skin testifying to a life in the sun, working with his hands, moving about, sharing with all who intersect his path. I am one who crossed his path, a convert, a believer in the God who can change a hippie into a prophet.

Setting the book down, I notice a large box by the wall...

FROM TERRI.

My sister gives such big gifts. A giver. An achiever. A success. Probably a box of Gap clothes, a sharp tie, a pillow hand stitched in her spare time. Terri strives for the best.

A gift from the achiever.

Bright blonde hair, green eyes, white smile like a TV anchorwoman. Independent from the start. No help needed. Faced with a challenge, she'll take it, overcome it, or go around it. The lawyer, the spokeswoman, the leader. Give me Terri in a courtroom, in a jam, in a battle anytime. A warrior.

And a child. Sensitive, softened by hurt. Married young, divorced, unable to have children, the one barren in a home full of kids, babies, and cries, her own cries over the one miscarriage that closed her womb forever. Now the independent one holds tightly to her family. She pours her energy, her passion into us, into me. I sense her love. I love her strength, the strength to emerge from an unfair battle with grace instead of hate.

Moving to the other side of the tree I find a gift overshadowed by a large card...

FROM JAN.

A practical gift. Simple. Nothing extra. Basic, but needed. With a card detailing the gift's importance and my need to appreciate it.

Words from the teacher.

The smart one. The valedictorian, standing straight, decked in gold, speaking to her classmates with confidence, eloquence. The college grad. The chemistry major, able to grasp the complexities of ions, eons, and neons. A paradox. A cheerleader. A social dater—John the Pothead, Billy the Athlete, Jim the Success. The searcher for truth, for direction.

Now the mother of eight well-disciplined, bright, obedient children who say "Yes, ma'am" and "No, sir" to questions from adults. The teacher still teaching but a different subject, God's truth, the emptiness of success, the black-and-white of issues, with confidence, eloquence. Still a paradox. Giggling and dogmatic. Confident and self-conscious. Chemistry major and stay-at-home mother of eight.

I look for a present next to Jan's. It must be there, somewhere, always beside Jan, but I can't find it. It must be gone...

FROM JILL.

My heart aches. The void under the tree a microcosm of the void in my heart. Tears stream down my cheeks and drip on the carpet where a gift should be but isn't, for a sister who should be here but isn't.

The absence of the saint.

Petite, frail, timid, beautiful. The quiet one, no words, no pretense, no striving for the spotlight. The follower.

With Jan. Two sisters. Siamese twins attached at the heart. Jan the leader, Jill the follower. Cheerleaders together, roommates, soulmates. Jan the valedictorian, Jill the salutatorian.

With Lee. Boyfriend and girlfriend. High school sweethearts. True love. Every prom picture together. A drawing of "Lee n' Jill" etched in pencil, interlocking, proportionate, simple letters transformed into a piece of art. A bride, dressed in white with no contradiction. The unity candle designed for their love. A mother of two boys. "Boys will be boys." But not around Jill. Energetic bounce-off-the-walls boys tempered by the quiet, strong, faithful love of their mother.

With Christ. Cancer victim. Bald head, sunken cheeks, tan skin paled to a green tint. Heavy eyes, unable to walk, yet able to smile, to encourage, to change the heart of a self-sufficient father to faith in the All-Sufficient Father. A saint. A martyr, steadfastly testifying to the comfort of Christ in the fires of life in this sin-cursed, heartless world, not worthy to contain the life of one so precious, so pure. Faithful to the end. Christ the Leader, Jill the follower.

Grief still present, still strong, I must think about something else. I rummage around the mound of gifts for something different, strange. I find it. Wrapped in colorful paper filled with cross-eyed reindeer, monster elves, and a pot-bellied Santa Claus on a recliner watching soaps, this gift can only be from one person…

FROM ROB.

I have no idea what to expect. A box of switches, a bag of coal, a handcrafted birdhouse, a pair of underwear embedded with rhinestones…

A surprise from the prodigal.

A rebel. An almost criminal. Too smart to be caught, riding the line between the legal and the illegal, the prank and the felony. The evil older brother, melting my army men, shooting my toys with his BB gun, giving his beloved younger brother an ample supply of thumps, noogies, and wedgies. Dating the glamorous, the blondes, the dancers, the kissers. Attracting them with his boyish grin, his carved muscles, his chrome-wheeled, freshly waxed Mustang. Radio blaring out rock music, fishtailing down dirt roads, unafraid of pain, of death. Wowing the girls, impressing the guys, tormenting his brother, who is petrified in the backseat with fingers stuck in his ears. My scream of "I hate you, Rob!" met with satisfaction.

But the prodigal came home. Empty, humble, kneeling by the couch at 2 A.M., he prayed with me. "Lord, forgive me of my many sins…" New life. New relationships. New identity.

A husband. Grinning from ear to ear, holding the hand of Brandi as I read the vows.

"Rob, do you take this woman as your lawfully wedded wife?"

"I do."

The stud settles down.

A father. Videotaping his baby daughter, little Jill, remembering his sister in the innocence of a newborn. Sensitive, sincere, saved. The rebel cradles his child in big hands turned soft.

A brother. In the flesh and in the Spirit. A new creation. A witness of God's amazing grace. My words, "I love you, Rob," met with satisfaction. Sinner turned saint. The prodigal come home.

The living room is now alive with activity. My dad sits in the corner, under a lamp, reading his Bible. Mom works tirelessly in the kitchen. The smell of bacon and eggs saturating the air. My brothers and sisters arrive with children, with smiles. Holding hands around the table, unified in spirit, sharers of eternal life.

My dad offers our thanks to God for His provision of food, for the hope of seeing Jill again, for the gift of Jesus Christ, our Savior. While my dad prays, I open my eyes and peer around the table. I see the faces of those who have shaped my life, formed my memories, taught me to love. Each one a unique thread woven into my life, adding color, strength, and wholeness. They are my foundation, my safety net, my roots, my blessing, my gift…

FROM GOD.[60]

[60] Steven Foster, "A Message, a Word, an Achiever, a Surprise," *Kindred Spirit,* vol. 22, no. 4, Winter 1998.

Made in the USA
Columbia, SC
04 July 2019